A VEIN OF MOCKERY

A Vein
of Mockery

TWENTIETH-CENTURY VERSE SATIRE

Chosen and

Introduced

by

JAMES REEVES

HEINEMANN

LONDON

Heinemann Educational Books Ltd

LONDON EDINBURGH MELBOURNE AUCKLAND TORONTO
HONG KONG SINGAPORE KUALA LUMPUR
IBADAN NAIROBI JOHANNESBURG
NEW DELHI

ISBN 0 435 14769 2

Introduction and arrangement © James Reeves 1973
First published 1973

Published by
Heinemann Educational Books Ltd
48 Charles Street, London W1X 8AH
Printed in Great Britain by Morrison and Gibb Ltd
London and Edinburgh

CONTENTS

v

To Keith Nettle

INTRODUCTION

POETRY in Britain and America shuns definition and evades categories. No satisfactory definition of satire exists, so that an anthologist may, within certain limits, be as exclusive or as inclusive as he thinks fit. To call it, as one writer has, 'writing which expresses a sense of amusement or disgust excited by the ridiculous or the unseemly', for instance, leaves a large body of genuine satire out of account. While the history of a literary term is not always of much help in defining it at any given period, in the case of satire a brief reference to its origin is appropriate in the present century. Satire seems to have started as a rude and crude form of invective used at popular festivals. A slanging match between rival factions or individuals under the influence of the festive spirit was the foundation of satire when it was taken up by literary writers. The writer referred to regards humour as an essential element in satire: without it, he considers satire to be mere invective. But I am inclined to think that it need have no humour and may well be little more than invective expressed in literary form. A slanging match between two London taxi-drivers or Irish political antagonists may be satirical, though it is unlikely to be expressed in verse. Nor can we take very seriously Sir Philip Sidney's reference in his *Defence of Poesy* to being 'rhymed to death, as is said to be done in Ireland'. On the other hand, there is vigour and artistry in the verse 'flytings' (formal exchanges of abuse, often lengthy and often scurrilous) such as those between late medieval Scots poets – for instance, Dunbar and William Kennedy. These are certainly an early form of satire. The word itself was invented by the Latin poets, not by their Greek forerunners, and comes from a word meaning a full flagon of wine, and thence a full measure of assorted matter. 'Saturae' had their origin, so far as Italy is concerned, in the festivals accompanying the wine harvest. What began as spirited expressions of personal or communal animosity were developed by literary writers, notably Horace, Persius, Martial and Juvenal, as a means of commenting on public events or private vices.

In England there have been two ages of satire in the classical sense. Donne, Hall and Marston were the principal satirists of the late sixteenth and early seventeenth centuries, at a time when satire co-existed with lyric poetry. Andrew Marvell wrote both, but with him lyric poetry came temporarily to an end, and the second great age of satire – that of Dryden, Swift and Pope – held sway. Satire dominated the field until it was overshadowed by the new romantic poetry of the later eighteenth century. From then on, satire has been spasmodic in England, never dying out entirely, but never holding the leading place, even in the work of a single poet. Moreover, the development of prose as a vehicle of satiric criticism, going back to the great prose satires of Swift, has channelled the satiric spirit away from verse. Verse, indeed, from the Romantics onwards, has tended to be regarded as too important, too numinous for anything as secondary in importance as satire. Indeed, only in the time of Dryden and Pope has satirical verse been accorded the principal place in English literature. One has only to mention Byron as the one considerable writer of satirical verse in the Romantic period, to realize that his form had suffered a more or less permanent eclipse by his time. If Byron had been born a century earlier, he would undoubtedly have been a major verse satirist (thus incurring the wrath of his rival Pope, whom in his own day he greatly admired and energetically defended against his Romantic detractors). But fashion was too much for Byron, so that satire remains a minor component of his poetry, taken as a whole.

One need only name Shelley and Tennyson, who both wrote an occasional satirical poem, to realize that, in English poetry during the nineteenth century satire had deserted serious poetry, appearing later in prose writers such as Thackeray and Samuel Butler.

In the twentieth century we reach a period when the whole literary and social climate has been completely different from the last great age of satire. Freedom of speech and the press, absence of political censorship, have made satire for political ends unnecessary. Why extract amusement from differences in political thinking when you can express them in forthright denunciations in the press and the other media? In this respect verse satire has declined since the time of Pope. In another respect, too, the age is different. Personal exchanges as those between Pope and his detractors and rivals are not in the spirit of twentieth-century social customs.

Nevertheless, the last fifty years have been, in some ways, an age of satire comparable with the age of Pope. Satirical controversy, however, has mainly been expressed in prose and latterly in the theatre, with which I am not here concerned. But the satirical spirit has prevailed, and has been expressed in the form of vigorous and telling verse, usually embedded in the writings of poets better known for their non-satirical work. Very few, if any, modern poets have earned a reputation solely, or even principally, as satirists. For this reason if for no other, I have thought it worth while, and found it of very great interest, to compile an anthology of satire, in this way exposing a vein of mockery which lies below the surface of modern poetry and is sometimes overlooked. No one thinks of Hardy, Yeats, de la Mare or Graves principally as satirists; it would be wrong to do so. But all are represented here. A poet is, if he is anything at all, a whole man, having all the emotions and moods of men: anger or contempt aroused in the most lyrical or the most gentle of poets by something he regards as wrong may on occasions stir him to satiric utterance.

The very absence, since the Romantic period, of an accepted tradition of verse satire has left poets free to be satirical about anyone and anything in whatever form they find most appropriate. Verse satire may be a marginal activity in the twentieth century, but it has a lively and persistent being under the surface

3

of what is regarded as predictable poetic activity. The fact that no one is, as it were, *expected* to compose satire means that the quality of satire, when it is manifested, is high. For my part, I consider that certain poets who may prefer, or have preferred, to be regarded chiefly for non-satire are at their most felicitous in this vein: MacNeice for one, Sassoon for another, and among living poets I would add the names of William Plomer and Henry Reed – though this is to cast no reflection on their other poems, which I value highly.

It follows, too, that the moods and motives behind satire are extremely varied. Religious cant, humbug of all kinds, suburban respectability, eccentricity in behaviour and opinions, social snobbery, the evils of bureaucratic rule – all these have excited poets to anger, contempt or amusement. So have the monstrosity of war and the sad fact of cruelty to animals. I hope that one feature of this anthology which will be appreciated is its variety. Almost every aspect of modern life receives attention, from private love to global war.

What, then, is satire? In avoiding a rigid definition I hope to focus attention on the actual verse selected for this book, and so to make, or to suggest, a pragmatic approach. To begin with, it is obviously a *critical* activity: it criticizes society and the individual in all their aspects. The critical spirit may derive either from a genuine desire to reform by ridicule or contempt, or from motives as personal as spite or envy. It is perhaps for this later reason that satire is regarded as a comparatively low form of poetry. We have learnt, since the time of Pope, to be tolerant. We try to extract pleasure and amusement from the follies of society rather than castigate them. There are of course exceptions: no one would think of Walter de la Mare, who has been compared with the 'gentle-hearted' Charles Lamb, as a natural satirist. But when he was moved to anger, as by war and cruelty and the corruption of the innocent, he wrote powerful and moving satire – satire so serious that some would deny it the name. But I call it satire because its anger, its very seriousness, must carry over to the reader in the form of an anger which, in the aggregate, must help the cause of reform.

To write critically of any phenomenon, a poet must, at any rate temporarily, be in an objective state of mind: he cannot write effective satire if he is wholly engrossed in his own feelings and reactions. Absorption with his own psyche is inimical to the spirit of satire. At the other end of the scale from the anger of Sassoon or de la Mare is the almost affectionate ridicule of literary parody – an effective branch of satire in the field of literary criticism. The best parody is written *con amore*: but the love which makes a poet parody another must be temporarily suspended while the victim's faults are exposed. It is this detachment which makes it possible for a poet to attend to the craft and technique of his verse; only this will make the results pleasing to read, memorable and repeatable. I am inclined to think that the major purpose of satire in this century has been to entertain, to give pleasure through humour and skilled writing. This, I fear, is the reason why, the further my researches into the poetry of those under, say, forty have taken me, the more difficult it has been to find satirical verse worthy to stand with the best of the older writers. The last twenty-five years, like the eighteenth century, have been deficient in the poetic spirit, and it might be expected, therefore, that there would have been a corresponding growth in satire. But on the whole the younger poets simply do not have the technique to write good satire. Their writing is often too slapdash, their rhythms too careless, their diction too 'instant', to make their social criticism effective. It can readily be admitted that they are socially involved – 'committed', as the word goes – but only commitment to poetry, which is a total commitment, can serve to make them write the technically good, as distinct from casual and exhibitionistic, verse, even on a comparatively unambitious level which reinforces social criticism. It is no slight on a poet to say that he cannot write satire: he may not want to, or he may be of too subjective a nature to wish to attempt it. I have searched the poems of some excellent twentieth-century poets in vain for satire.

Not only is this an anthology of varied moods, it is one of varied tones and styles. The urbane Betjeman is as different from the rough-tongued D. H. Lawrence as possible. Indeed, Lawrence seems to me to get as near as anyone to the direct kind of utterance sought less successfully by some younger, socially conscious writers of today. Writing in his own explosive and irritable free verse, he also gets farther away, some would think, from true satire than any poet who should be represented here. I have felt justified in including him because of the broadness of my definition: he writes invective in almost the primitive sense. Technically his poems are far from artless and reveal a good ear for the rhythms of common speech, an instinct for economy of expression, an almost uncanny feeling for the right word.

It need hardly be said that I do not identify myself with every point of view expressed here. Some poems are manifestly unfair; some are even mean-spirited; some are reactionary in outlook. But there is a place for everything in satire, and this is perhaps why an age so various as the last fifty years has done it well. Apart from satiric intent, the only criterion that has guided me has been that of literary quality, including the capacity to offer an interest beyond the immediate occasion of the poem. There is a good deal of skilful and amusing verse – or there was until recently – included in reviews and sketches for the stage and other entertainment media; but it dates too quickly, it is too topical. Good satire must be more than merely topical, or at least it must have enough humour or other entertainment value, to make it worth while for the reader to look up a note explaining where the poem is not self-explanatory, the occasion of its first appearance. No doubt the film epics of the late Cecil B. de Mille are already a fading memory, but Nicholas Bentley's neat and inspired clerihew will be read long after the films are seen by living audiences.

Two questions may occur to the reader of this anthology. First, can satire be poetry? Is it poetry of an inferior sort, or not poetry at all? Secondly, can satire ever be effective as an instrument for change? I will give briefly my personal thoughts on these questions. There can certainly be *great* satire, to use a deliberately indefinable term. Swift wrote great prose satire, as did Molière in dramatic verse. Swift also wrote very good verse satire, but I don't know that it ought to be called poetry. Dryden wrote great satire; Pope wrote very effective satire. But in the last analysis I would not call either *Absalom and Achitophel* or the *Epistle to Dr Arbuthnot* poetry in its true sense. I repeat that this is a personal view. There is a sense in which, say, Pope's portrait of Sporus is very good, perhaps even great, satire. But this may be for a reason unsuspected by Pope himself. For it could be argued that in writing of Sporus he was writing not about Lord Hervey, but about himself. He rose above satire into a region almost of unconscious self-revelation. One important motive for satire is the expiation of private guilt by attacking or ridiculing one's own concealed errors or faults in the person of another. Some American poets, notably Cummings, have sought to expiate a national, rather than a personal, guilt in this way. Returning to the twentieth century, it seems to me that some of the poems in this selection are true poems, but in these cases the poetry may be said to subsume the satire. In other cases, too, the poem rises above its immediate occasion and transcends it, so that, in the sense in which such poems are about some large subjects, such as life itself, or happiness, or human nature, rather than society in any temporal sense, they can be read as poems. Perhaps this is to say no more than that poetry and satire merge into one another, and the boundary between them is not always clear to see.

Can satire be effective as an instrument for social change? Such change and such effectiveness can never, in the jargon of the day, be quantified. But it can, over a reasonably long period, be perceived. There is, for instance, undoubtedly less hypocrisy, less formality for form's sake today, than there was fifty years ago. We believe in plain speaking. We do not wrap up our prejudices and our feelings in empty words to the extent that was expected in ordinary social intercourse when I was young. There has been a change, and this has been brought about by a complex of causes, one of which is certainly the written word. Satirical verse, if it has no direct or immediate influence for change, is part of the general traffic in words which influences attitudes. It is also a cement to the freemasonry which exists between people of like mind in the various matters with which it is concerned. But I do not think social change is the paramount purpose of satire today

7

(if indeed it ever was). As I have said, I think it is a far from contemptible entertainment activity – harmless at worst, enlightening and nourishing at best. This is not primarily a collection of humorous poems, but I hope much humour will be found here – a commodity which we are in danger of being short of.

J. R.

Lewes, 1972

I

Politics —— Religion —— War

The Scholars

Bald heads forgetful of their sins,
Old, learned, respectable bald heads
Edit and annotate the lines
That young men, tossing on their beds,
Rhymed out in love's despair
To flatter beauty's ignorant ear.

All shuffle there; all cough in ink;
All wear the carpet with their shoes;
All think what other people think;
All know the man their neighbour knows.
Lord, what would they say
Did their Catullus walk that way?

                                    W. B. YEATS

'When statesmen gravely say'

When statesmen gravely say – 'We must be realistic –'
The chances are they're weak and therefore pacifistic:
But when they speak of Principles – look out – perhaps
Their generals are already poring over maps.

                                    W. H. AUDEN

Marginalia

Unable to see
a neighbour to frown at,
Eutroplus beat his wife.
        (*after Conrad Lorenz*)

Justice: permission to peck
a wee bit harder
than we have been pecked.

★   ★   ★

In semi-literate countries
demogogues pay
court to teenagers.

★   ★   ★

The tyrant's device:
*Whatever Is Possible
Is Necessary.*

★   ★   ★

Patriots? Little boys,
obsessed by Bigness,
Big Pricks, Big Money, Big Bangs.

★   ★   ★

The tobacco farmers
were Baptists who considered
smoking a sin.

W. H. AUDEN

On the Birth of his Son

Families, when a child is born,
Want it to be intelligent.
I, through intelligence,
Having wrecked my whole life,
Only hope the baby will prove
Ignorant and stupid.
Then he will crown a tranquil life
By becoming a Cabinet Minister.

ARTHUR WALEY

from the Chinese of SU TUNG-P'O (1036–1101)

a politician

> a politician is an arse upon
> which everyone has sat except a man
>
> e. e. cummings

On Reading the War Diary of a Defunct Ambassador

So that's your Diary – that's your private mind
Translated into shirt-sleeved History. That
Is what diplomacy has left behind
For after-ages to peruse, and find
What passed beneath your elegant silk-hat.

You were a fine old gentleman; compact
Of shrewdness, charm, refinement and finesse.
Impeccable in breeding, taste and dress,
No diplomatic quality you lacked –
No tittle of ambassadorial tact.

I can imagine you among 'the guns',
Urbanely peppering partridge, grouse, or pheasant –
Guest of those infinitely privileged ones
Whose lives are padded, petrified, and pleasant.
I visualize you feeding off gold plate
And gossiping on grave affairs of State.

Now you're defunct; your gossip's gravely printed;
The world discovers where you lunched and dined
On such and such a day; and what was hinted
By ministers and generals far behind
The all-important conflict, carnage-tinted.

The world can read the rumours that you gleaned
From various Fronts; the well-known Names you met;
Each conference you attended and convened;
And (at appropriate moments) what you ate.
Thus (if the world's acute) it can derive
Your self, exact, uncensored and alive.

The world will find no pity in your pages;
No exercise of spirit worthy of mention;
Only a public-funeral grief-convention;
And all the circumspection of the ages.
But I, for one, am grateful, overjoyed,
And unindignant that your punctual pen
Should have been so constructively employed
In manifesting to unprivileged men
The visionless officialized fatuity
That once kept Europe safe for Perpetuity.

SIEGFRIED SASSOON

' next to of course god '

'next to of course god america i
love you land of the pilgrims' and so forth oh
say can you see by the dawn's early my
country 'tis of centuries come and go
and are no more what of it we should worry
in every language even deafanddumb
thy sons acclaim your glorious name by gorry
by jingo by gee by gosh by gum
why talk of beauty what could be more beaut-
iful than these heroic happy dead
who rushed like lions to the roaring slaughter
they did not stop to think they died instead
then shall the voice of liberty be mute?'

He spoke. And drank rapidly a glass of water.

e. e. cummings

At the Bank in Spain

Even the old priest, in his long black robe and silvery hair
came to the counter with his hat off, humble at the shrine,
and was immensely flattered when one of the fat little
    clerks of the bank
shook hands with him.

D. H. LAWRENCE

The Mosquito Knows —

The mosquito knows full well, small as he is
he's a beast of prey.
But after all
he only takes his bellyful,
he doesn't put my blood in the bank.

D. H. LAWRENCE

Wages

The wages of work is cash.
The wages of cash is want more cash.
The wages of want more cash is vicious competition.
The wages of vicious competition is – the world we live in.

The work-cash-want circle is the viciousest circle
that ever turned men into fiends.

15

Earning a wage is a prison occupation
and a wage-earner is a sort of gaol-bird.
Earning a salary is a prison overseer's job,
a gaoler instead of a gaol-bird.

Living on your income is strolling grandly outside the
      prison
in terror lest you have to go in. And since the work-prison
      covers
almost every scrap of the living earth, you stroll up and
      down
on a narrow beat, about the same as a prisoner taking his
      exercise.

This is called universal freedom.

D. H. LAWRENCE

A Civil Servant

While in this cavernous place employed
    Not once was I aware
Of my officious other-self
    Poised high above me there,

My self reversed, my rage-less part,
    A slimy yellowish cone –
Drip, drip; drip, drip – so down the years
    I stalagmized in stone.

Now pilgrims to the cave, who come
    To chip off what they can,
Prod me with child-like merriment:
    'Look, look! It's like a man!'

ROBERT GRAVES

A Tribute to the Founder

By bluster, graft, and doing people down
Sam Baines got rich, but, mellowing at last,
Felt that by giving something to the town
He might undo the evils of his past.

His hope was to prevent the local youth
From making the mistakes that he had made:
Choosing expediency instead of truth,
And quitting what was honest for what paid.

A university seemed just the thing,
And that old stately home the very place.
Sam wept with pleasure at its opening.
He died too soon to weep at its disgrace.

Graft is refined among the tea and scones,
Bluster (new style) invokes the public good,
And doing-down gets done in pious tones
Sam had tried to put on, but never could.

KINGSLEY AMIS

Planning Permission

He looked at me without surprise or pleasure
But with a bored, habitual compassion.
'They sent me here,' I said. 'I want to build.'
'Naturally,' he said. 'We'll see what we can do.'
Along the hopeless counter twenty others
Were seeing what they could do.
                              'You'll need these forms.'
Application for permission for an erection
For occupation as residential accommodation
And/or private domestic habitation.

'In triplicate of course. Return when filled
To the assistant sub-divisional officer.'
I took the papers. Tears of gratitude
Misted my sight; but he was gone already
Into the wastes beneath his sandy hair.

A year later I took the papers back.
Alone in his little room
The assistant sub-divisional officer sent for me.
He looked at me without surprise or pleasure
But with compassionate unrecognition.
'Permission for an erection. Quite so. We'll write.'
'Oh thank you, sir,' I started. 'Do you think . . . ?'
But under the sandy hair the eyes were blank.
After eleven months the answer came.
'Rejection of permission for an erection.
Any appeal to be directed within three years
To the sub-divisional officer for attention.'

Two years and more went by before I gained
The sub-divisional officer's section. With relief
I saw that he at least had had his due reward.
Between the flat ears under the greying hair
No sign of recognition stirred.
                              'Ah yes.
Objection to rejection of application for erection.'
With the old bored compassion in his voice,
'We'll do,' he promised, 'what we can to help.'
'Oh sir,' I sobbed. He interrupted me.
'I'll pass on your objection to the divisional officer.
It may take time.'
                    Re-charged with hope I went.

I died; and here I falter by the gate
Drained of desire and too ashamed to face
The sorrowing figure on the throne of grace.

JAMES REEVES

18

Was it not Curious?

Was it not curious of Aúgustin
Saint Aúgustin, Saint Aúgustin,
When he saw the beautiful British children
To say such a curious thing?

He said he must send the gospel, the gospel,
At once to them over the waves
He never said he thought it was wicked
To steal them away for slaves

To steal the children away
To buy and have slavery at all
Oh no, oh no, it was not a thing
That caused him any appal.

Was it not curious of *Gregory*
Rather more than of Aúgustin?
It was not curious so much
As it was wicked of them.

STEVIE SMITH

The Hippopotamus

*Similiter et omnes revereantur Diaconos, ut man-
datum Jesu Christi; et Episcopum, ut Jesum Christum,
existentem filium Patris; Presbyteros autem, ut
concilium Dei et conjunctionem Apostolorum. Sine
his Ecclesia non vocatur; de quibus suadeo vos
sic habeo.*

S. IGNATII AD TRALLIANOS

*And when this epistle is read among you, cause that
it be read also in the church of the Laodiceans.*

The broad-backed hippopotamus
Rests on his belly in the mud;
Although he seems so firm to us
He is merely flesh and blood.

Flesh and blood is weak and frail,
Susceptible to nervous shock;
While the True Church can never fail
For it is based upon a rock.

The hippo's feeble steps may err
In compassing material ends,
While the True Church need never stir
To gather in its dividends.

The 'potamus can never reach
The mango on the mango-tree;
But fruits of pomegranate and peach
Refresh the Church from over sea.

At mating time the hippo's voice
Betrays inflexions hoarse and odd,
But every week we hear rejoice
The Church, at being one with God.

The hippopotamus's day
Is passed in sleep; at night he hunts;
God works in a mysterious way –
The Church can sleep and feed at once.

I saw the 'potamus take wing
Ascending from the damp savannas,
And quiring angels round him sing
The praise of God in loud hosannas.

Blood of the Lamb shall wash him clean
And him shall heavenly arms enfold,

Among the saints he shall be seen
Performing on a harp of gold.

He shall be washed as white as snow,
By all the martyr'd virgins kist,
While the True Church remains below
Wrapt in the old miasmal mist.

T. S. ELIOT

In Church

'And now to God the Father,' he ends,
And his voice thrills up to the topmost tiles:
Each listener chokes as he bows and bends,
And emotion pervades the crowded aisles.
Then the preacher glides to the vestry-door,
And shuts it, and thinks he is seen no more.

The door swings softly ajar meanwhile,
And a pupil of his in the Bible class,
Who adores him as one without gloss or guile,
Sees her idol stand with a satisfied smile
And re-enact at the vestry-glass
Each pulpit gesture in deft dumb-show
That had moved the congregation so.

THOMAS HARDY

In the Cemetery

'You see those mothers squabbling there?'
Remarks the man of the cemetery.
'One says in tears, " 'Tis mine lies here!"
Another, "Nay, mine, you Pharisee!"

Another, *"How dare you move my flowers*
And put your own on this grave of ours!"
But all their children were laid therein
At different times, like sprats in a tin.

'And then the main drain had to cross,
And we moved the lot some nights ago,
And packed them away in the general foss
With hundreds more. But their folks don't know,
And as well cry over a new-laid drain
As anything else, to ease your pain!'

THOMAS HARDY

Cambridge

Imagine all the dons in the attitudes of buggers
With their complicated neurotic simplicity of learning,
Something comfortable, something not quite real,
The life of the tea-table, the book-scattered study,
The manuscript under the magnifying glass
In that white, cultured hand, deserving of pity.

Dons live on with occasional satisfaction,
Hand on the shoulder of a promising pupil,
Attracted but envious of the coming young men,
Middle age has caught them and the night comes on,
No soothing books and no charming companions
To quieten those nerves that cry for satisfaction.

What was their desire? Was it known and never realized,
Behind the lines and bathed in yellow lamplight?
In the world where their young men fight and are wounded
They suffer neglect like a curtain or a picture.
Pitying themselves they are never wounded,
Suffering quietly with a book in hand or smoking.

GAVIN EWART

Founder's Feast

Old as a toothless Regius Professor
Ebbed the Madeira wine. Loquacious graduates
Sipped it with sublimation. They'd been drinking
The health of . . . was it Edward the Confessor?
A solemn banquet glowed in every cheek,
While nicotinean fumes befogged the roof
And the carved gallery where prim choristers
Sang like Pre-Raphaelite angels through the reek.

Gowns, rose and scarlet in flamingo ranks,
Adorned the dais that shone with ancient silver;
And guests of honour gazed far down the Hall
With precognition of returning thanks.
There beamed the urbanest Law-lord on the Bench,
Debating with the Provost (ceremonious
In flushed degrees of vintage scholarship),
The politics of Plato, – and the French.

But on the Provost's left, in gold and blue,
Sat . . . O my God ! . . . great Major-General Bluff . . .
Enough enough enough enough enough !

SIEGFRIED SASSOON

What Schoolmasters Say

What schoolmasters say is not always wrong.
'You're a good chap, Smiggers, but don't go to seed'
Said Pettitt in bathtime at school long ago.
He seemed so earnest that I nearly cried;
But up until now I've laughed at his warning
Of where disregard of his words might lead –
Until last night when I dreamed I had died
And Pettitt was God.

Hank made us lay out our beds like soldiers;
After Cert. 'A' he summoned me, scowling
'Vile boy, I see that you've mucked it again!'
Of course, I didn't care then: I was proud
And resigned from the Corps against his advice –
But heard Hank's voice with its military sting
As today I strode through the playground crowd:
        'Well, Smith, you've failed!'

I pity myself that now I'm a puppet
Like Hank, and Pettitt, and roaring Gubbo;
That I must answer, when asked by my friends
'If you take your pupils aside and say:
'Vile boys, this won't do, disobedience is wrong,
And if you don't know it I'll make you know!'
Do you *really* mean that those boys should obey?':
        'I may, in a way.'

They are singing this morning before me
'How wonderful' etc. 'must thy sight be'
And if their croaking cannot quite mean God
Nor can it quite mean me. I ask myself: what
Should it mean? Their heads incline; I bow
My own, until a colleague warns: 'Hey, old
Boy! Head up, and watch for talking: *we're* not
        Expected to pray!'
                                    MARTIN SEYMOUR-SMITH

The Eugenist

Come, human dogs, interfertilitate –
    Blackfellow and white lord, brown, yellow and red!
Accept the challenge of the lately bred
    Newfoundland terrier with the dachshund gait.

Breed me gigantic pygmies, meek-eyed Scots,
  Phlegmatic Irish, perfume-hating Poles,
Poker-faced, toothy, pigtailed Hottentots,
  And Germans with no envy in their souls.

ROBERT GRAVES

Songs of Education

III. FOR THE CRÊCHE

Form 8277059, Sub-Section K

I remember my mother, the day that we met,
A thing I shall never entirely forget;
And I toy with the fancy that, young as I am,
I should know her again if we met in a tram.
  But mother is happy in turning a crank
  That increases the balance at somebody's bank;
  And I feel satisfaction that mother is free
  From the sinister task of attending to me.

They have brightened our room, that is spacious
      and cool,
With diagrams used in the Idiot School,
And Books for the Blind that will teach us to see;
But mother is happy, for mother is free.
  For mother is dancing up forty-eight floors,
  For love of the Leeds International Stores,
  And the flame of that faith might perhaps have
      grown cold,
  With the care of a baby of seven weeks old.

For mother is happy in greasing a wheel
For somebody else, who is cornering Steel;
And though our one meeting was not very long,

She took the occasion to sing me this song:
  'O, hush thee, my baby, the time will soon come
  When thy sleep will be broken with hooting and
      hum;
  There are handles want turning and turning all day,
  And knobs to be pressed in the usual way;

  O, hush thee, my baby, take rest while I croon,
  For Progress comes early, and Freedom too soon.'
                                     G. K. CHESTERTON

Apollo of the Physiologists

Despite this learned cult's official
And seemingly sincere denial
That they either reject or postulate
God, or God's scientific surrogate,
Prints of a deity occur *passim*
Throughout their extant literature. They make him
A dumb, dead-pan Apollo with a profile
Drawn in Victorian-Hellenistic style –
The pallid, bald, partitioned head suggesting
Wholly abstract cerebral functioning;
Or nude and at full length, this deity
Displays digestive, venous, respiratory
And nervous systems painted in bold colour
On his immaculate exterior.
Sometimes, *in verso*, a bald, naked Muse,
His consort, flaunts her arteries and sinews,
While, upside-down, crouched in her chaste abdomen,
Adored by men and wondered at by women,
Hangs a Victorian-Hellenistic foetus –
Fruit of her academic god's afflatus.
                                     ROBERT GRAVES

Base Details

If I were fierce, and bald, and short of breath,
  I'd live with scarlet Majors at the Base,
And speed glum heroes up the line to death.
  You'd see me with my puffy petulant face,
Guzzling and gulping in the best hotel,
  Reading the Roll of Honour. 'Poor young chap,'
I'd say – 'I used to know his father well;
  Yes, we've lost heavily in this last scrap.'
And when the war is done and youth stone dead,
I'd toddle safely home and die – in bed.

SIEGFRIED SASSOON

Does it Matter?

Does it matter? – losing your legs? . . .
For people will always be kind,
And you need not show that you mind
When the others come in after hunting
To gobble their muffins and eggs.

Does it matter? – losing your sight? . . .
There's such splendid work for the blind;
And people will always be kind,
As you sit on the terrace remembering
And turning your face to the light.

Do they matter? – those dreams from the pit? . . .
You can drink and forget and be glad,
And people won't say that you're mad;
For they'll know you've fought for your country
And no one will worry a bit.

SIEGFRIED SASSOON

27

'They'

The Bishop tells us: 'When the boys come back
'They will not be the same; for they'll have fought
'In a just cause: they lead the last attack
'On Anti-Christ; their comrades' blood has bought
'New right to breed an honourable race,
'They have challenged Death and dared him face to face.'

'We're none of us the same!' the boys reply.
'For George lost both his legs; and Bill's stone blind;
'Poor Jim's shot through the lungs and like to die;
'And Bert's gone syphilitic; you'll not find
'A chap who's served that hasn't found *some* change.'
And the Bishop said: 'The ways of God are strange!'

SIEGFRIED SASSOON

The Persian Version

Truth-loving Persians do not dwell upon
The trivial skirmish fought near Marathon.
As for the Greek theatrical tradition
Which represents that summer's expedition
Not as a mere reconnaissance in force
By three brigades of foot and one of horse
(Their left flank covered by some obsolete
Light craft detached from the main Persian fleet)
But as a grandiose, ill-starred attempt
To conquer Greece – they treat it with contempt;
And only incidentally refute
Major Greek claims, by stressing what repute
The Persian monarch and the Persian nation
Won by this salutary demonstration:
Despite a strong defence and adverse weather
All arms combined magnificently together.

ROBERT GRAVES

Lessons of the War

Vixi duellis nuper idoneus
Et militavi non sine gloria

I. NAMING OF PARTS

Today we have naming of parts. Yesterday,
We had daily cleaning. And tomorrow morning,
We shall have what to do after firing. But today,
Today we have naming of parts. Japonica
Glistens like coral in all of the neighbouring gardens,
    And today we have naming of parts.

This is the lower sling swivel. And this
Is the upper sling swivel, whose use you will see,
When you are given your slings. And this is the piling swivel,
Which in your case you have not got. The branches
Hold in the gardens their silent, eloquent gestures,
    Which in our case we have not got.

This is the safety-catch, which is always released
With an easy flick of the thumb. And please do not let me
See anyone using his finger. You can do it quite easy
If you have any strength in your thumb. The blossoms
Are fragile and motionless, never letting anyone see
    Any of them using their finger.

And this you can see is the bolt. The purpose of this
Is to open the breech, as you see. We can slide it
Rapidly backwards and forwards: we call this
Easing the spring. And rapidly backwards and forwards
The early bees are assaulting and fumbling the flowers:
    They call it easing the Spring.

They call it easing the Spring: it is perfectly easy
If you have any strength in your thumb: like the bolt,

And the breech, and the cocking-piece, and the point of balance,
Which in our case we have not got; and the almond-blossom
Silent in all of the gardens and the bees going backwards and
    forwards,
    For today we have naming of parts.

II. JUDGING DISTANCES

Not only how far away, but the way that you say it
Is very important. Perhaps you may never get
The knack of judging a distance, but at least you know
How to report on a landscape: the central sector,
The right of arc and that, which we had last Tuesday,
    And at least you know.

That maps are of time, not place, so far as the army
Happens to be concerned – the reason being,
Is one which need not delay us. Again, you know
There are three kinds of tree, three only, the fir and the poplar,
And those which have bushy tops to them; and lastly
    That things only seem to be things.

A barn is not called a barn, to put it more plainly,
Or in a field in the distance, where sheep may be safely grazing.
You must never be over-sure. You must say, when reporting:
At five o'clock in the central sector is a dozen
Of what appears to be animals; whatever you do,
    Don't call the bleeders *sheep*.

I am sure that's quite clear; and suppose, for the sake of example,
The one at the end, asleep, endeavours to tell us
What he sees over there to the west, and how far away,
After first having come to attention. There to the west,
On the fields of summer the sun and the shadows bestow
    Vestments of purple and gold.

The still white dwellings are like a mirage in the heat,
And under the swaying elms a man and a woman
Lie gently together. Which is, perhaps, only to say
That there is a row of houses to the left of arc,
And that under some poplars a pair of what appear to be humans
    Appear to be loving.

Well that, for an answer, is what we might rightly call
Moderately satisfactory only, the reason being,
Is that two things have been omitted, and those are important.
The human beings, now: in what direction are they,
And how far away, would you say? And do not forget
    There may be dead ground in between.

There may be dead ground in between; and I may not have got
The knack of judging a distance; I will only venture
A guess that perhaps between me and the apparent lovers,
(Who, incidentally, appear by now to have finished,)
At seven o'clock from the houses, is roughly a distance
    Of about one year and a half.

IV. MOVEMENT OF BODIES

Those of you that have got through the rest, I am going to rapidly
Devote a little time to showing you, those that can master it,
A few ideas about tactics, which must not be confused
With what we call strategy. Tactics is merely
The mechanical movement of bodies, and that is what we mean
    by it.
    Or perhaps I should say: by them.

Strategy, to be quite frank, you will have no hand in.
It is done by those up above, and it merely refers to
The larger movements over which we have no control.
But tactics are also important, together or single.
You must never forget that suddenly, in an engagement,
    You may find yourself alone.

31

This brown clay model is a characteristic terrain
Of a simple and typical kind. Its general character
Should be taken in at a glance, and its general character
You can see at a glance it is somewhat hilly by nature,
With a fair amount of typical vegetation
     Disposed at certain parts.

Here at the top of the tray, which we might call the northwards,
Is a wooded headland, with a crown of bushy-topped trees on;
And proceeding downwards, or south, we take in at a glance
A variety of gorges and knolls and plateaus and basins and saddles,
Somewhat symmetrically put, for easy identification.
     And here is our point of attack.

But remember of course it will not be a tray you will fight on,
Nor always by daylight. After a hot day, think of the night
Cooling the desert down, and you still moving over it:
Past a ruined tank or a gun, perhaps, or a recently dead friend,
Lying about somewhere: it might quite well be that.
     It isn't always a tray.

And even this tray is different to what I had thought.
These models are somehow never always the same; the reason
I do not know how to explain quite. Just as I do not know
Why there is always someone at this particular lesson
Who always starts crying. Now will you kindly
     Empty those blinking eyes?

I thank you. I have no wish to seem impatient.
I know it is all very hard, but you would not like,
To take a simple example, to take for example,
This point I have mentioned here, you would not like
To find yourself face to face with it, and you not knowing
     What there might be inside?

Very well then: suppose this is what you must capture.
It will not be easy, not being very exposed,

Secluded away like it is, and somewhat protected
By a typical formation of what appear to be bushes,
So that you cannot see, as to what is concealed inside,
        As to whether it is friend or foe.

And so, a strong feint will be necessary in this connection.
It will not be a tray, remember. It may be a desert stretch
With nothing in sight, to speak of. I have no wish to be
        inconsiderate,
But I see there are two of you now, commencing to snivel.
I cannot think where such emotional privates can come from.
        Try to behave like men.

I thank you. I was saying: a thoughtful deception
Is always somewhat essential in such a case. You can see
That if only the attacker can capture such an emplacement
The rest of the terrain is his: a key-position, and calling
For the most resourceful manoeuvres. But that is what tactics is.
        Or should I say rather: are.

Let us begin then and appreciate the situation.
I am thinking especially of the point we have been considering,
Though in a sense everything in the whole of the terrain
Must be appreciated. I do not know what I have said
To upset so many of you. I know it is a difficult lesson.
        Yesterday a man was sick,

But I have never known as many as *five* in a single intake,
Unable to cope with this lesson. I think you had better
Fall out, all five, and sit at the back of the room,
Being careful not to talk. The rest will close up.
Perhaps it was me saying 'a dead friend', earlier on?
        Well, some of us live.

And I never know why, whenever we get to tactics,
Men either laugh or cry, though neither being strictly called for.
But perhaps I have started too early with a difficult problem?

We will start again, further north, with a simpler assault.
Are you ready? Is everyone paying attention?
    Very well, then. Here are two hills.

HENRY REED

The Flying Bum: 1944

In the vegetarian guest-house
All was frolic, feast and fun,
Eager voices were inquiring
'Are the nettle cutlets done?'
Peals of vegetarian laughter,
Husky wholesome wholemeal bread –
Will the evening finish with a
Rush of cocoa to the head?

Yes, you've guessed; it's Minnie's birthday,
Hence the frolic, hence the feast.
Are there calories in custard?
There are vitamins in yeast.
Kate is here and Tom her hubby,
Ex-commissioner for oaths,
She is mad on Christian Science,
Parsnip flan he simply loathes.

And Mr Croaker, call him Arthur,
Such a keen philatelist,
Making sheep's-eyes at Louisa
(After dinner there'll be whist) –
Come, sit down, the soup is coming,
All of docks and darnels made,
Drink a health to dear old Minnie
In synthetic lemonade.

Dentures champing juicy lettuce,
Champing macerated bran,
Oh the imitation rissoles!
Oh the food untouched by man!
Look, an imitation sausage
Made of monkey-nuts and spice,
Prunes tonight and semolina,
Wrinkled prunes, unpolished rice.

Yards of guts absorbing jellies,
Bellies filling up with nuts,
Carbo-hydrates jostling proteins
Out of intestinal ruts;
Peristalsis calls for roughage,
Haulms and fibres, husks and grit,
Nature's way to open bowels,
Maybe – let them relish it.

'Hark, I hear an air-raid warning!'
'Take no notice, let 'em come.'
'Who'll say grace?' 'Another walnut?'
'Listen, what's that distant hum?'
'Bomb or no bomb,' stated Minnie,
'Lips unsoiled by beef or beer
We shall use to greet our Maker
When he sounds the Great All-Clear.'

When the flying bomb exploded
Minnie's wig flew off her pate,
Half a curtain, like a tippet,
Wrapped itself round bony Kate,
Plaster landed on Louisa,
Tom fell headlong on the floor,
And a spurt of lukewarm custard
Lathered Mr Croaker's jaw.

All were spared by glass and splinters
But, the loud explosion past,

Greater was the shock impending
Even than the shock of blast –
Blast we veterans know as freakish
Gave this feast its final course,
Planted bang upon the table
A lightly roasted rump of horse.

WILLIAM PLOMER

Dry August Burned

Dry August burned. A harvest hare
Limp on the kitchen table lay,
Its fur blood-blubbered, eyes astare,
While a small child that stood near by
Wept out her heart to see it there.

Sharp came the *clop* of hoofs, the clang
Of dangling chain, voices that rang.
Out like a leveret she ran,
To feast her glistening bird-clear eyes
On a team of field artillery,
Gay, to manoeuvres, thudding by.
Spur and gun and limber plate
Flashed in the sun. Alert, elate,
Noble horses, foam at lip,
Harness, stirrup, holster, whip,
She watched the sun-tanned soldiery,
Till dust-white hedge had hidden away –
Its din into a rumour thinned –
The laughing, jolting, wild array:
And then – the wonder and tumult gone –
Stood nibbling a green leaf, alone,
Her dark eyes, dreaming. . . . She turned, and ran,
Elf-like, into the house again.

The hare had vanished. . . . 'Mother,' she said,
Her tear-stained cheek now flushed with red,
'Please, may I go and see it skinned?'

WALTER DE LA MARE

II

Society — Love — Sex — Marriage

How beastly the bourgeois is

How beastly the bourgeois is
especially the male of the species –

Presentable eminently presentable –
shall I make you a present of him?

Isn't he handsome? isn't he healthy? Isn't he a fine specimen?
doesn't he look the fresh clean englishman, outside?
Isn't it god's own image? tramping his thirty miles a day
after partridges, or a little rubber ball?
wouldn't you like to be like that, well off, and quite the thing?

Oh, but wait!
Let him meet a new emotion, let him be faced with another
    man's need,
let him come home to a bit of moral difficulty, let life face
    him with a new demand on his understanding
and then watch him go soggy, like a wet meringue.
Watch him turn into a mess, either a fool or a bully.
Just watch the display of him, confronted with a new demand
    on his intelligence,
a new life-demand.

How beastly the bourgeois is
especially the male of the species—

Nicely groomed, like a mushroom
standing there so sleek and erect and eyeable –
and like a fungus, living on the remains of bygone life
sucking his life out of the dead leaves of greater life than his own.

And even so, he's stale, he's been there too long.
Touch him, and you'll find he's all gone inside
just like an old mushroom, all wormy inside, and hollow
under a smooth skin and an upright appearance.

Full of seething, wormy, hollow feelings
rather nasty –
How beastly the bourgeois is!

Standing in their thousands, these appearances, in damp England
what a pity they can't all be kicked over
like sickening toadstools, and left to melt back, swiftly
into the soil of England.

D. H. LAWRENCE

Humanity i love you

Humanity i love you
because you would rather black the boots of
success than enquire whose soul dangles from his
watch-chain which would be embarrassing for both

parties and because you
unflinchingly applaud all
songs containing the words country home and
mother when sung at the old howard

Humanity i love you because
when you're hard up you pawn your
intelligence to buy a drink and when
you're flush pride keeps

you from the pawn shop and
because you are continually committing

nuisances but more
especially in your own house

Humanity i love you because you
are perpetually putting the secret of
life in your pants and forgetting
it's there and sitting down

on it
and because you are
forever making poems in the lap
of death Humanity

i hate you

e. e. cummings

The World State

Oh, how I love Humanity,
　　With love so pure and pringlish,
And how I hate the horrid French,
　　Who never will be English!

The International Idea,
　　The largest and the clearest,
Is welding all the nations now,
　　Except the one that's nearest.

This compromise has long been known,
　　This scheme of partial pardons,
In ethical societies
　　And small suburban gardens –

The villas and the chapels where
I learned with little labour
The way to love my fellow-man
And hate my next-door neighbour.

G. K. CHESTERTON

The Firm of Happiness Limited

The firm of Happiness, Limited, was one to astonish the stars,
More like a thriving town than a multiple store – a hotchpotch
Of markets and playrooms and chapels and brothels and baths
     and bars,
As smoothly running and closely packed as the works of a watch.

Nobody finally understood the cause of the crash.
Some spoke of Nemesis; others rumoured, vaguely, of course,
That a gang of Directors had simply robbed the firm of its cash,
Or that some ironical Jew was selling it short on the Bourse.

Whatever the reason, the firm of a sudden began to fail.
The floors were undusted at corners, the commissionaires were
     unshaved,
The girls were anxious and raucous, the comedian's jokes were
     stale.
The customers noticed the difference – to judge from the way
     they behaved.

When Happiness closed its doors, the Corporation of the city
Were distressed to see so vast a property left alone
To moulder and waste; in a mingled impulse of thrift and pity
They decided to buy the empty building, and floated a loan.

Now nobody knows what to do with this monstrous hulk we
     have bought.

At the last Corporation meeting one alderman, half in jest,
Spoke of turning it into a barracks. Meanwhile there's the dreary
    thought
That we ratepayers have to keep paying the burdensome interest.

NORMAN CAMERON

The Dorking Thigh

About to marry and invest
Their lives in safety and routine
Stanley and June required a nest
And came down on the 4.15.

The agent drove them to the Posh Estate
And showed them several habitations.
None did. The afternoon got late
With questions, doubts, and explanations.

Then day grew dim and Stan fatigued
And disappointment raised its head,
But June declared herself intrigued
To know where that last turning led.

It led to a Tudor snuggery styled
'Ye Kumfi Nooklet' on the gate.
'A gem of a home,' the salesman smiled,
'My pet place on the whole estate;

'It's not quite finished, but you'll see
Good taste itself.' They went inside.
'This little place is built to be
A husband's joy, a housewife's pride.'

They saw the white convenient sink,
The modernistic chimneypiece,
June gasped for joy, Stan gave a wink
To say, 'Well, here our quest can cease.'

The salesman purred (he'd managed well)
And June undid a cupboard door.
'For linen,' she beamed. And out there fell
A nameless Something on the floor.

'Something the workmen left, I expect,'
The agent said, as it fell at his feet,
Nor knew that his chance of a sale was wrecked.
'Good heavens, it must be a joint of meat!'

Ah yes, it was meat, it was meat all right,
A joint those three will never forget –
For they stood alone in the Surrey night
With the severed thigh of a plump brunette . . .

★ ★ ★

Early and late, early and late,
Traffic was jammed round the Posh Estate,
And the papers were full of the Dorking Thigh
And who, and when, and where, and why.

A trouser button was found in the mud
(Who made it? Who wore it? Who lost it?
        Who knows?)
But no one found a trace of blood
Or her body or face, or the spoiler of those.

He's acting a play in the common air
On which no curtain can ever come down.
Though 'Ye Kumfi Nooklet' was shifted elsewhere
June made Stan take a flat in town.

WILLIAM PLOMER

The Oxford Voice

When you hear it languishing
and hooing and cooing and sidling through the front teeth,
    the oxford voice
      or worse still
    the would-be oxford voice
you don't even laugh any more, you can't.
For every blooming bird is an oxford cuckoo nowadays,
you can't sit on a bus nor in the tube
but it breathes gently and languishingly in the back of your neck.

And oh, so seductively superior, so seductively
    self-effacingly
    deprecatingly
      superior. –
We wouldn't insist on it for a moment
    but we are
      we are
    you admit we are
      superior.——

D. H. LAWRENCE

How to Get On in Society

Originally set as a competition in 'Time and Tide'

Phone for the fish-knives, Norman
    As Cook is a little unnerved;
You kiddies have crumpled the serviettes
    And I must have things daintily served.

Are the requisites all in the toilet?
    The frills round the cutlets can wait

Till the girl has replenished the cruets
    And switched on the logs in the grate.

It's ever so close in the lounge, dear,
    But the vestibule's comfy for tea
And Howard is out riding on horseback
    So do come and take some with me.

Now here is a fork for your pastries
    And do use the couch for your feet;
I know what I wanted to ask you –
    Is trifle sufficient for sweet?

Milk and then just as it comes dear?
    I'm afraid the preserve's full of stones;
Beg pardon, I'm soiling the doileys
    With afternoon tea-cakes and scones.
                    JOHN BETJEMAN

The Feckless Dinner-Party

'Who are we waiting for?' '*Soup* burnt?' '. . . Eight – '
    'Only the tiniest party. – Us!'
'Darling! Divine!' 'Ten minutes late – '
    'And my digest – ' 'I'm *rav*enous!'
' "Toomes"?' – 'Oh, he's new.' 'Looks crazed, I guess.'
    ' "Married" – *Again!*' 'Well; more or less!'

'Dinner is *served!*' ' "Dinner is served"!'
    'Is served?' 'Is served.' 'Ah, yes.'

'Dear Mr Prout, will you take down
    The Lilith in leaf-green by the fire?
Blanche Ogleton? . . .' 'How coy a frown! –
    Hasn't she borrowed *Eve's* attire?'

'Morose Old Adam!' 'Charmed – I vow.'
'Come then, and meet her now.'

'Now, Dr Mallus – would you please? –
Our daring poetess, Delia Seek?'
'The lady with the bony knees?'
'And – *entre nous* – less song than beak.'
'Sharing her past with Simple Si – '
'*Bare* facts! He'll blush!' 'Oh, fie!'

'And *you*, Sir Nathan – false but fair! –
That fountain of wit, Aurora Pert.'
'More wit than It, poor dear! But there . . .'
'Pitiless Pacha! *And* such a flirt!'
' "Flirt"! *Me?*' 'Who else?' 'You here. . . . Who can . . .?'
'In*corr*igible man!'

'And now, Mr Simon – little me! –
Last and – ' 'By no means least!' 'Oh, come!
What naughty, naughty flattery!
Honey! – I *hear* the creature hum!'
'Sweets for the sweet, *I* always say!'
' "Always"? . . . We're last.' '*This* way?' . . .

'No, sir; straight on, please.' 'I'd have vowed! –
I came the other . . .' 'It's queer; I'm sure . . .'
'What frightful pictures!' 'Fiends!' 'The *crowd!*'
'Such nudes!' 'I can't endure . . .'

'Yes, *there* they go.' 'Heavens! *Are* we right?'
'Follow up closer!' ' "Prout"? – sand-blind!'
'This endless . . .' 'Who's turned down the light?'
'Keep calm! They're close behind.'

'Oh! Dr Mallus; what dismal stairs!'
'I hate these old Victor . . .' 'Dry rot!'

'Darker and darker!' 'Fog!' 'The air's . . .'
  'Scarce breathable!' 'Hell!' '*What?*'

'The banister's gone!' 'It's deep; keep close!'
  'We're going down and down!' 'What fun!'
'Damp! Why, my shoes . . .' 'It's slimy . . . Not *moss!*'
  'I'm freezing cold!' 'Let's run.'

'. . . Behind us. I'm giddy. . . .' 'The catacombs . . .'
  'That shout!' 'Who's there?' 'I'm *alone!*' 'Stand back!'
'She said Lead . . .' 'Oh!' 'Where's Toomes?' '*Toomes!*' 'Toomes!'
  'Stifling!' 'My skull will crack!'

'Sir Nathan! *Ai!*' 'I *say*! *Toomes!* Prout!'
  'Where? Where?' ' "Our silks and fine array" . . .'
'She's mad.' 'I'm dying!' 'Oh, Let me *out!*'
  'My God! We've lost our way!' . . .

And now how sad-serene the abandoned house,
Whereon at dawn the spring-tide sunbeams beat;
And time's slow pace alone is ominous,
And naught but shadows of noonday therein meet;
Domestic microcosm, only a Trump could rouse:
And, pondering darkly, in the silent rooms,
He who misled them all – the butler, Toomes.

                                    WALTER DE LA MARE

The British Workman and the Government

Hold my hand, Auntie, Auntie,
Auntie, hold my hand!
I feel I'm going to be naughty, Auntie,
and you don't seem to understand.

Hold my hand and love me, Auntie,
love your little boy!
We want to be loved, especially, Auntie,
us whom you can't employ.

Idle we stand by the kerb-edge, Auntie,
dangling our useless hands.
But we don't mind so much if you love us, and we feel
that Auntie understands.

                                      D. H. LAWRENCE

Chico and the Prison Doctors

a few months ago a friend of mine named Chico
was kicked in his groin by a promotion hungry
policeman and since then my friend has sporadically had
severe pains in above mentioned region which
stops him walking or even standing so he saw
our prison doctor two weeks ago who then sent
to the prison out patients hospital since then
he has had six urine samples taken and three
blood same in the end he got a little worried
concerning the efficiency of these silent doctors
so he refused the fourth blood sample and asked
for help please so they gave him some medicine

six weeks ago I was given the same medicine
as Chico only they gave it to me then as a
TREATMENT FOR WHOOPING COUGH!!

Signed Tim and Chico

                                      TIM DALY

A Ballad of the Good Lord Nelson

The Good Lord Nelson had a swollen gland,
Little of the scripture did he understand
Till a woman led him to the promised land
    Aboard the Victory, Victory O.

Adam and Evil and a bushel of figs
Meant nothing to Nelson who was keeping pigs,
Till a woman showed him the various rigs
    Aboard the Victory, Victory O.

His heart was softer than a new laid egg,
Too poor for loving and ashamed to beg,
Till Nelson was taken by the Dancing Leg
    Aboard the Victory, Victory O.

Now he up and did up his little tin trunk
And he took to the ocean on his English junk,
Turning like the hour-glass in his lonely bunk
    Aboard the Victory, Victory O.

The Frenchman saw him a-coming there
With the one-piece eye and the valentine hair,
With the safety-pin sleeve and occupied air
    Aboard the Victory, Victory O.

Now you all remember the message he sent
As an answer to Hamilton's discontent –
There were questions asked about it in Parliament
    Aboard the Victory, Victory O.

Now the blacker the berry, the thicker comes the juice.
Think of Good Lord Nelson and avoid self-abuse,
For the empty sleeve was no mere excuse
    Aboard the Victory, Victory O.

'England Expects' was the motto he gave
When he thought of little Emma out on Biscay's wave,
And remembered working on her like a galley-slave
    Aboard the Victory, Victory O.

The first Great Lord in our English land
To honour the Freudian command,
For a cast in the bush is worth two in the hand
    Aboard the Victory, Victory O.

Now the Frenchman shot him there as he stood
In the rage of battle in a silk-lined hood
And he heard the whistle of his own hot blood
    Aboard the Victory, Victory O.

Now stiff on a pillar with a phallic air
Nelson stylites in Trafalgar Square
Reminds the British what once they were
    Aboard the Victory, Victory O.

If they'd treat their women in the Nelson way
There'd be fewer frigid husbands every day
And many more heroes on the Bay of Biscay
    Aboard the Victory, Victory O.

                    LAWRENCE DURRELL

The Ruined Maid

'O 'Melia, my dear, this does everything crown!
Who could have supposed I should meet you in Town?
And whence such fair garments, such prosperi-ty?' –
'O didn't you know I'd been ruined?' said she.

– 'You left us in tatters, without shoes or socks,
Tired of digging potatoes, and spudding up docks;

And now you've gay bracelets and bright feathers three!' –
'Yes: that's how we dress when we're ruined,' said she.

– 'At home in the barton you said 'thee' and 'thou',
And 'thik oon', and 'theäs oon', and 't'other'; but now
Your talking quite fits 'ee for high compa-ny' –
'Some polish is gained with one's ruin,' said she.

– 'Your hands were like paws then, your face blue and bleak
But now I'm bewitched by your delicate cheek,
And your little gloves fit as on any la-dy!' –
'We never do work when we're ruined,' said she.

– 'You used to call home-life a hag-ridden dream,
And you'd sigh, and you'd sock; but at present you seem
To know not of megrims or melancho-ly!' –
'True. One's pretty lively when ruined,' said she.

– 'I wish I had feathers, a fine sweeping gown,
And a delicate face, and could strut about Town!' –
'My dear – a raw country girl, such as you be,
Cannot quite expect that. You ain't ruined,' said she.

THOMAS HARDY

The Conformers

Yes; we'll wed, my little fay,
    And you shall write you mine,
And in a villa chastely gray
    We'll house, and sleep, and dine
      But those night-screened, divine,
    Stolen trysts of heretofore,
We of choice ecstasies and fine
      Shall know no more.

The formal faced cohue
Will then no more upbraid
With smiting smiles and whisperings two
Who have thrown less loves in shade.
We shall no more evade
The searching light of the sun,
Our game of passion will be played,
Our dreaming done.

We shall not go in stealth
To rendezvous unknown
But friends will ask me of your health,
And you about my own.
When we abide alone,
No leapings each to each,
But syllables in frigid tone
Of household speech.

When down to dust we glide
Men will not say askance,
As now: 'How all the country side
Rings with their mad romance!'
But as they graveward glance
Remark: 'In them we lose
A worthy pair, who helped advance
Sound parish views.'

THOMAS HARDY

The Lady in the Furs

'I'm a lofty lovely woman,'
Says the lady in the furs,
In the glance she throws around her
On the poorer dames and sirs:

'This robe, that cost three figures,
    Yes, is mine,' her nod avers.

'True, my money did not buy it,
    But my husband's, from the trade;
And they, they only got it
    From things feeble and afraid
By murdering them in ambush
    With a cunning engine's aid.

'True, my hands, too, did not shape it
    To the pretty cut you see,
But the hands of midnight workers
    Who are strangers quite to me:
It was fitted, too, by dressers
    Ranged around me toilsomely.

'But I am a lovely lady,
    Though sneerers say I shine
By robbing Nature's children
    Of apparel not mine,
And that I am but a broom-stick,
    Like a scarecrow's wooden spine.'
                    THOMAS HARDY

Hi!

Hi! handsome hunting man
Fire your little gun.
Bang! Now the animal
Is dead and dumb and done.
Nevermore to peep again, creep again, leap again,
Eat or sleep or drink again, Oh, what fun!
                    WALTER DE LA MARE

The Habits

When they put him in rompers the habits
Fanned out to close in, they were dressed
In primary colours and each of them
Carried a rattle and a hypodermic;
His parents said it was all for the best.

Next, the barracks of boys: the habits
Slapped him on the back, they were dressed
In pinstripe trousers and carried
A cheque book, a passport, and a sjambok;
The master said it was all for the best.

And then came the women: the habits
Pretended to leave, they were dressed
In bittersweet undertones and carried
A Parthian shaft and an affidavit;
The adgirl said it was all for the best.

Age became middle: the habits
Made themselves at home, they were dressed
In quilted dressing-gowns and carried
A decanter, a siphon, and a tranquillizer;
The computer said it was all for the best.

Then age became real: the habits
Outstayed their welcome, they were dressed
In nothing and carried nothing.
He said: If you won't go, I go.
The Lord God said it was all for the best.

LOUIS MACNEICE

Request on the Field

When I was broken down and unemployed
You found me bitter, wry and under-joyed.
I would not pay my licences or dues,
To vote I did improperly refuse.
So captain-like my shoulder-blade you smote
And cried: 'Up lad! Cast off your sullen coat
And (after you have registered your vote)
Get on the pitch among the knaves and fools
And play the game according to their rules –
They're doing, after all, what you won't do.
Respect them then. Later love comes, too.'

I heeded your wise words, and now am on the field
With shirt and socks and red-cross shield.
But before you dribble off, at captain's call,
Could you explain the absence of a ball?

MARTIN SEYMOUR-SMITH

III

Cranks — America and Other Places

Death of an Actress

I see from the paper that Florrie Forde is dead –
Collapsed after singing to wounded soldiers,
At the age of sixty-five. The American notice
Says no doubt all that need be said

About this one-time chorus girl; whose rôle
For more than forty stifling years was giving
Sexual, sentimental, or comic entertainment,
A gaudy posy for the popular soul.

Plush and cigars: she waddled into the lights,
Old and huge and painted, in velvet and tiara,
Her voice gone but around her head an aura
Of all her vanilla-sweet forgotten vaudeville nights.

With an elephantine shimmy and a sugared wink
She threw a trellis of Dorothy Perkins roses
Around an audience come from slum and suburb
And weary of the tea-leaves in the sink;

Who found her songs a rainbow leading west
To the home they never had, to the chocolate Sunday
Of boy and girl, to cowslip time, to the never-
Ending weekend Islands of the Blest.

In the Isle of Man before the war before
The present one she made a ragtime favourite
Of 'Tipperary', which became the swan-song
Of troop-ships on a darkened shore;

And during Munich sang her ancient quiz
Of *Where's Bill Bailey?* and the chorus answered,

Muddling through and glad to have no answer:
Where's Bill Bailey? How do *we* know where he is!

Now on a late and bandaged April day
In a military hospital Miss Florrie
Forde has made her positively last appearance
And taken her bow and gone correctly away.

Correctly. For she stood
For an older England, for children toddling
Hand in hand while the day was bright. Let the wren and robin
Gently with leaves cover the Babes in the Wood.

LOUIS MACNEICE

The Playboy of the Demi-World: 1938

Aloft in Heavenly Mansions, Doubleyou One –
Just Mayfair flats, but certainly sublime –
You'll find the abode of D'Arcy Honeybunn,
A rose-red sissy half as old as time.

Peace cannot age him, and no war could kill
The genial tenant of those cosy rooms,
He's lived there always and he lives there still,
Perennial pansy, hardiest of blooms.

There you'll encounter aunts of either sex,
Their jokes equivocal or over-ripe,
Ambiguous couples wearing slacks and specs
And the stout Lesbian knocking out her pipe.

The rooms are crammed with flowers and objets d'art,
A Ganymede still hands the drinks – and plenty!
D'Arcy still keeps a rakish-looking car
And still behaves the way he did at twenty.

A ruby pin is fastened in his tie,
The scent he uses is *Adieu Sagesse*,
His shoes are suede, and as the years go by
His tailor's bill's not getting any less.

He cannot whistle, always rises late,
Is good at indoor sports and parlour tricks,
Mauve is his favourite colour, and his gait
Suggests a peahen walking on hot bricks.

He prances forward with his hands outspread
And folds all comers in a gay embrace,
A wavy toupee on his hairless head,
A fixed smile on his often-lifted face.

'My dear!' he lisps, to whom all men are dear,
'How perfectly enchanting of you!'; turns
Towards his guests and twitters, 'Look who's here!
Do come and help us fiddle while Rome burns!'

'The kindest man alive,' so people say,
'Perpetual youth!' But have you seen his eyes?
The eyes of some old saurian in decay
That asks no questions and is told no lies.

Under the fribble lurks a worn-out sage
Heavy with disillusion, and alone;
So never say to D'Arcy, 'Be your age!' –
He'd shrivel up at once or turn to stone.

WILLIAM PLOMER

Slough

Come, friendly bombs, and fall on Slough
It isn't fit for humans now,

63

There isn't grass to graze a cow
      Swarm over, Death!

Come, bombs, and blow to smithereens
Those air-conditioned, bright canteens,
Tinned fruit, tinned meat, tinned milk, tinned beans
      Tinned minds, tinned breath.

Mess up the mess they call a town –
A house for ninety-seven down
And once a week a half a crown
      For twenty years,

And get that man with double chin
Who'll always cheat and always win,
Who washes his repulsive skin
      In women's tears.

And smash his desk of polished oak
And smash his hands so used to stroke
And stop his boring dirty joke
      And make him yell.

But spare the bald young clerks who add
The profits of the stinking cad;
It's not their fault that they are mad,
      They've tasted Hell.

It's not their fault they do not know
The birdsong from the radio,
It's not their fault they often go
      To Maidenhead.

And talk of sports and makes of cars
In various bogus Tudor bars
And daren't look up and see the stars
      But belch instead.

In labour-saving homes, with care
Their wives frizz out peroxide hair
And dry it in synthetic air
    And paint their nails.

Come, friendly bombs, and fall on Slough
To get it ready for the plough.
The cabbages are coming now:
    The earth exhales.

c. 1937   JOHN BETJEMAN

'¡ Wellcome, to the Caves of Artá!'

'*They are hollowed out in the see coast at the muncipal terminal of
Capdepera, at nine kilometer from the town of Artá in the Island of
Mallorca, with a suporizing infinity of graceful colums of 21 meter and
by downward, wich prives the spectator of all animacion and plunges
in dumbness. The way going is very picturesque, serpentine between
style mountains, til the arrival at the esplanade of the vallee called
'The Spider'. There are good enlacements of the railroad with auto-
buses of excursion, many days of the week, today actually Wednesday
and Satturday. Since many centuries renown foreing visitors have
explored them and wrote their eulogy about, included Nort-American
geoglogues.*'   [From a Tourist leaflet]

Such subtile filigranity and nobless of construccion
    Here fraternize in harmony, that respiracion stops.
While all admit their impotence (though autors most formidable)
    To sing in words the excellence of Nature's underprops,
Yet stalactite and stalagmite together with dumb language
    Make hymns to God wich celebrate the strength of water drops.

¿You, also, are you capable to make precise in idiom
    Consideracions magic of ilusions very wide?

Alraedy in the Vestibule of these Grand Caves of Artá
  The spirit of the human verb is darked and stupefyed;
So humildy you trespass trough the forest of the colums
  And listen to the grandess explicated by the guide.

From darkness into darkness, but at measure, now descending
  You remark with what esxactitude he designates each bent;
'The Saloon of Thousand Banners', or 'The Tumba of Napoleon',
  'The Grotto of the Rosary', 'The Club', 'The Camping Tent'.
And at 'Cavern of the Organ' there are knocking streange
        formacions
  Wich give a nois particular pervoking wonderment.

¡ Too far do not adventure, sir! For, further as you wander,
  The every of the stalactites will make you stop and stay.
Grand peril amenaces now, your nostrills aprehending
  An odour least delicious of lamentable decay.
It is some poor touristers, in the depth of obscure cristal,
  Wich deceased of thier emocion on a past excursion day.

                                        ROBERT GRAVES

Welcome to Wales

Come to Wales
To be buried; the undertaker
Will arrange it for you. We have
The sites and a long line
Of clients going back
To the first milkman who watered
His honour. How they endow
Our country with their polished
Memorials! No one lives
In our villages, but they dream
Of returning from the rigours

Of the pound's climate. Why not
Try it? We can always raise
Some mourners, and the amens
Are ready. This is what
Chapels are for; their varnish
Wears well and will go
With most coffins. Let us
Quote you; our terms
Are the lowest, and we offer,
Dirt cheap, a place where
It is lovely to lie.

R. S. THOMAS

Aberdarcy: the Main Square

By the new Boots, a tool-chest with flagpoles
Glued on, and flanges, and a dirty great
Baronial doorway, and things like port-holes,
Evans met Mrs Rhys on their first date.

Beau Nash House, that sells Clothes for Gentlemen,
Jacobethan, every beam nailed on tight –
Real wood, though, mind you – was in full view when,
Lunching at the Three Lamps, she said all right.

And he dropped her beside the grimy hunk
Of castle, that with luck might one day fall
On to the *Evening Post*, the time they slunk
Back from that lousy week-end in Porthcawl.

The journal of some bunch of architects
Named this the worst town centre they could find;
But how disparage what so well reflects
Permanent tendencies of heart and mind?

All love demands a witness: something 'there'
Which it yet makes part of itself. These two
Might find Carlton House Terrace, St Mark's Square,
A bit on the grand side. What about you?

KINGSLEY AMIS

Resort

The sea flicks its spray over it.
Occasionally a high tide
Swills its cellars. For the rest
There are only the few streets
With the boredom of their windows.
People, people: the erect species
With its restlessness and the need to pay –
What have they come here to find?
Must they return to the vomit
Of the factories? On the conveyor belt
Of their interests they circle the town
To emerge jaded at the pier;
To look at the water with dull eyes
Resentfully, not understanding
A syllable. Did they expect
The sea, too, to be bi-lingual?

R. S. THOMAS

No Offence

In no country
Are the disposal services more efficient.

Standardized dustbins
Fit precisely into the mouth of a large cylinder
Slung on a six-wheeled chassis.
Even the dustbin lid is raised mechanically
At the very last moment.
You could dispose of a corpse like this
Without giving the least offence.

In no country
Are the public lavatories more immaculately kept.
As neat as new pins, smelling of pine forests,
With a roar like distant Wagner
Your sins are washed away.

In no country
Do the ambulances arrive more promptly.
You are lying on the stretcher
Before the police, the driver, the bystanders and the
                                neighbouring shopkeepers
Have finished lecturing you.

In no country
Are the burial facilities more foolproof.
A few pfennigs a week, according to age,
Will procure you a very decent funeral.
You merely sign on the dotted line
And keep your payments regular.

In no country
Are the disposal services more efficient
– I reflect –
As I am sorted out, dressed down, lined up,
Shepherded through the door,
Marshalled across the smooth-faced asphalt,
And fed into the mouth of a large cylinder
Labelled 'Lufthansa'.

D. J. ENRIGHT

The North

Living in the North one gets used to the cold nights
The cities, like stone tongues in the valleys
And the lugged crowds, daft zombies, poured through the streets.

The people are friendly enough, if you'll join them
In the Mecca Meat Market or the boozy clubs.
When you see the men at work as you walk through the cities
You think 'How wild, primitive, dirty and careless'
But when you talk to them in the pubs
You will find they like their jobs well enough,
Hand their wives money on a Friday
And respect the intellectual brother-in-law
Who is 'an accountant' or 'head of the costing department'.
Only the pox-bitten old reprobate, drunk in the corner,
Hands us the scraps of profanity we need for our working class
      novel.

They're not a bad lot, if you'll join them,
But if you judge them on what they say about queers and the
      work-shy
About sexual offenders generally, or even Teddy Boys shouting,
Then I suppose you would call them a bad lot.
You'd think they were puritanical till you hear their jokes
Or what they did to 'the dirty old pro's' with the army in Naples
And the ones who were in Egypt all know the same bit of Arabic.

At the end of it all you think 'They're just scared of the missus:
Or they like to think they're in the majority
– That's the reason they all defend democracy'

I don't call them a bad lot, but I watch my tongue
– Especially on Saturdays.

BRIAN HIGGINS

A Word in Edgeways

Tell me about yourself they
say and you begin to
tell them about yourself and
that is just the way I
am is their reply: they play
it all back to you in another
key, their key, and then in mid-
narrative they pay you a
compliment as if to say what a good
listener you are I am
a good listener my stay
here has developed my faculty I will
say that for me I will not
say that every literate male in
America is a soliloquist, a
ventriloquist, a strategic
egotist, an inveterate
campaigner-explainer over and
back again on the terrain of him-
self – what I will
say is they are not un-
interesting: they are simply
unreciprocal and yes it was a
pleasure if not an unmitigated
pleasure and I yes I did enjoy our
conversation goodnightthankyou

CHARLES TOMLINSON

Romance of a Youngest Daughter

Who will wed the Dowager's youngest daughter,
The Captain? filled with ale?

He moored his expected boat to a stake in the water
And stumbled on sea-legs into the Hall for mating,
Only to be seduced by her lady-in-waiting,
Round-bosomed, and not so pale.

Or the thrifty burgher in boots and fancy vest
With considered views of marriage?
By the tidy scullery maid he was impressed
Who kept that house from depreciation and dirt,
But wife does double duty and takes no hurt,
So he rode her home in his carriage.

Never the spare young scholar antiquary
Who was their next resort;
They let him wait in the crypt of the Old Library
And found him compromised with a Saxon book,
Claiming his truelove Learning kept that nook
And promised sweet disport.

Desirée (of a mother's christening) shall never wed
Though fairest child of her womb;
'We will have revenge,' her injured Ladyship said,
'Henceforth the tightest nunnery be thy bed
By the topmost stair! When the ill-bred lovers come
We'll say, She is not at home.'

JOHN CROWE RANSOM

An Importer

Mrs Someone's been to Asia.
What she brought back would amaze ye.
Bamboos, ivories, jades, and lacquers,
Devil-scaring firecrackers,
Recipes for tea with butter,

Sacred rigmaroles to mutter,
Subterfuge for saving faces,
A developed taste in vases,
Arguments too stale to mention
'Gainst American invention;
Most of all the mass production
Destined to prove our destruction.
What are telephones, skyscrapers.
Safety razors, Sunday papers,
But the silliest evasion
Of the truths we owe an Asian?
But the best of her exhibit
Was a prayer machine from Tibet
That by brook power in the garden
Kept repeating Pardon, pardon;
And as picturesque machinery
Beat a sundial in the scenery –
The most primitive of engines
Mass producing with a vengeance.
Teach those Asians mass production?
Teach your grandmother egg suction.

ROBERT FROST

come, gaze with me upon this dome

come, gaze with me upon this dome
of many coloured glass, and see
his mother's pride, his father's joy,
unto whom duty whispers low

'thou must!' and who replies 'I can!'
– yon clean upstanding well dressed boy
that with his peers full oft hath quaffed
the wine of life and found it sweet –

73

a tear within his stern blue eye,
upon his firm white lips a smile,
one thought alone: to do or die
for God for country and for Yale

above his blond determined head
the sacred flag of truth unfurled,
in the bright heyday of his youth
the upper class American

unsullied stands, before the world:
with manly heart and conscience free,
upon the front steps of her home
by the high minded pure young girl

much kissed, by loving relatives
well fed, and fully photographed
the son of man goes forth to war
with trumpets clap and syphilis

e. e. cummings

Americanization

Britannia needs no Boulevards,
   No spaces wide and gay:
Her march was through the crooked streets
   Along the narrow way.
Nor looks she where, New York's seduction,
The Broadway leadeth to destruction.

Britannia needs no Cafés:
   If Coffee needs must be,
Its place should be the Coffee-house
   Where Johnson growled for Tea;
But who can hear that human mountain
Growl for an ice-cream soda-fountain?

She needs no Russian Theatre,
   Where Father strangles Mother,
In scenes where all the characters
   And colours kill each other:
Her boast is freedom had by halves,
And Britons never shall be Slavs.

But if not hers the Dance of Death,
   Great Dostoievsky's dance,
And if the things most finely French
   Are better done in France –
Might not Americanization
Be best applied to its own nation?

Ere every shop shall be a store
   And every Trade a Trust . . .
Lo, many men in many lands
   Know when their cause is just.
There will be quite a large attendance
When *we* Declare our Independence.

G. K. CHESTERTON

IV

Poetry and the Arts

The Laureate

Like a lizard in the sun, though not scuttling
When men approach, this wretch, this thing of rage,
Scowls and sits rhyming in his horny age.

His time and truth he has not bridged to ours,
But shrivelled by long heliotropic idling
He croaks at us his out-of-date humours.

Once long ago here was a poet; who died.
See how remorse twitching his mouth proclaims
It was no natural death, but suicide.

Arrogant, lean, unvenerable, he
Still turns for comfort to the western flames
That glitter a cold span above the sea.

ROBERT GRAVES

Mr Nixon

In the cream gilded cabin of his steam yacht
Mr Nixon advised me kindly, to advance with fewer
Dangers of delay. 'Consider
        Carefully the reviewer.

'I was as poor as you are;
When I began I got, of course,
Advance on royalties, fifty at first,' said Mr Nixon,
'Follow me, and take a column,
Even if you have to work free.

'Butter reviewers. From fifty to three hundred
I rose in eighteen months;
The hardest nut I had to crack
Was Dr Dundas.

'I never mentioned a man but with the view
Of selling my own works.
The tip's a good one, as for literature
It gives no man a sinecure.

'And no one knows, at sight, a masterpiece.
And give up verse, my boy,
There's nothing in it.'

Likewise a friend of Bloughram's once advised me:
Don't kick against the pricks,
Accept opinion. The 'Nineties' tried your game
And died, there's nothing in it.

EZRA POUND

Museums

Museums offer us, running from among the buses,
A centrally heated refuge, parquet floors and sarcophaguses,
Into whose tall fake porches we hurry without a sound
Like a beetle under a brick that lies, useless, on the ground.

Warmed and cajoled by the silence the cowed cypher revives,
Mirrors himself in the cases of pots, paces himself by marble lives,
Makes believe it was he that was the glory that was Rome,
Soft on his cheek the nimbus of other people's martyrdom,
And then returns to the street, his mind an arena where sprawls
Any number of consumptive Keatses and dying Gauls.

LOUIS MACNEICE

The Apology of Bottom the Weaver

Once when an honest weaver slept,
  And Puck passed by, a kindly traitor,
And on his shoulders set the head
  Of a Shakespearean commentator,

The man had walked proverbial ways,
  Fair Science frowned not on his birth,
Nor lost in long and tangled dreams,
  The mother-wit of mother-earth.

Elaborate surgeons had not found
  The cobweb made the cure too brief,
Nor vegetarians taught the rule
  Of eating mustard without beef.

Only in that green night of growth
  Came to him, splendid, without scorn,
The lady of the dreams of men;
  The rival of all women born.

And he, for all his after weaving,
  Drew up from that abysmal dream
Immortal art, that proves by seeming
  All things more real than they seem.

The dancing moth was in his shuttle,
  The pea's pink blossom in his woof,
Your driving schools, your dying hamlets,
  Go through them all and find the proof –

That you, where'er the old crafts linger,
  Draw in their webs like nets of gold,
Hang up like banners for a pattern,
  The leavings of the looms of old.

And even as this home-made rhyme
  Drags but the speech of Shakespeare down,
These home-made patterns but repeat
  The traceries of an ancient clown.

And while the modern fashions fade,
  And while the ancient standards stream,
No psycho-analyst has knocked
  The bottom out of Bottom's dream.

G. K. CHESTERTON

Personality Cult

Instructions by a Celebrity for his Posthumous
Radio Portrait

When I am very dead, remember me,
But not the real me: leave that alone.
Call on the raddled dowager in Venice
And prop her up before a microphone.
My tamest jokes, most threadbare platitudes
She will retail in clichés all her own:
Then let the old bar bore pontificate
About my 'characteristic attitudes'.
Exhume the gardener; he will proudly boast
Of how I spoke to him as to a gent.
Let the world know how much my friendship meant
To the quack writer whom I hated most.
But above all, the ghosts of hostesses
At Georgian weekends, long in tooth and claw,
In tones as flat as oriental prints
Must quaveringly tell how on their lawns
In Berkshire, or amidst the Chelsea chintz,
I chatted literature with Bonar Law.

Say I was kind to animals and tradesmen;
Say how I lisped, and how my back-hair curled;
But do not say in Gath and Askelon
You bored me once and now you bore the world.

When I am very dead, remember me;
Let anything be told except the truth.
They didn't know me; I was no one's poodle
Vice made me man in age and fear in youth.

JAMES REEVES

Spicer's Instant Poetry

On sale everywhere: Spicer's Instant Poetry.
Trial size, 2/-; epic pack, 19/6.
A balanced mixture of clichés, catchwords,
Symbols, non sequiturs, ambiguities,
Stock phrases and borrowings from the best models.
Warranted free from superfluous emotion,
Bad rhymes and obvious plagiarism.
Simply add luke-warm milk and water.
A child can use it.
One teaspoonful reconstitutes a sonnet.
This infallible preparation
Makes poems suitable for competitions,
National and international festivals,
Private greetings cards and autograph albums.
Results guaranteed, and are to be seen
In best literary journals.
Spicer's Instant Poetry comes in seven popular shades:
Nature (including animals), childhood, domestic troubles,
Industry and politics, thwarted love,
Mythology and religion, foreign parts.
Special 'Parnassus' kit containing all the above varieties,

Free surprise item and coloured art portrait of leading bard,
Or 'Tartan Special' for Scottish subjects,
Five shillings only, post free.
Extra strong mix for homosexual or surgical pieces.
Delighted user writes: 'Instant Poetry
Is a joy for ever . . . Indistinguishable from the real thing.'
Order now and astonish your friends.
Big cash opportunities: Immortality
Assured or money returned.

JAMES REEVES

Bernard Shaw

Mr Bernard Shaw
Was just setting out for the war,
When he heard it was a dangerous trade
And demonstrably underpaid.

E. CLERIHEW BENTLEY

Survey of Literature

In all the good Greek of Plato
I lack my roast beef and potato.

A better man was Aristotle,
Pulling steady on the bottle.

I dip my hat to Chaucer,
Swilling soup from his saucer,

And to Master Shakespeare
Who wrote big on small beer.

The abstemious Wordsworth
Subsisted on a curd's-worth,

But a slick one was Tennyson,
Putting gravy on his venison.

What these men had to eat and drink
Is what we say and what we think.

The influence of Milton
Came wry out of Stilton.

Sing a song for Percy Shelley,
Drowned in pale lemon jelly,

And for precious John Keats,
Dripping blood of pickled beets.

Then there was poor Willie Blake,
He foundered on sweet cake.

God have mercy on the sinner
Who must write with no dinner,

No gravy and no grub,
No pewter and no pub,

No belly and no bowels,
Only consonants and vowels.
                    JOHN CROWE RANSOM

Generation of a Critic

The eager eye that went with you to school
Reported birds' eggs in the thicket;

The heart your mother and your father split
Was healed by girls and village cricket.

The euphuistic tongue and pen you practised
To gain no other recognition
Than that boon friend's you walked or drank beside.
Then Satan told you of ambition.

He whispered fame, wealth, power – and all that;
He promised honorary degrees;
He told you no one ever made a name
By cutting other names in trees.

So now the eager eye that went to school
With jealousy has gone a-squint;
The tongue is shrill, the ink turned poison,
Getting and keeping you in print.

JAMES REEVES

The Wicked Words

The wicked words corrupt. The young are gorged
On printed sex and violence till they tear
The pages up, still grunting with the urge
To rip a softer substance. Everywhere
The literate werewolves roam in drooling quest
Of nice white meat. Dread walks on pointed toes.
The wicked words corrupt, should be suppressed.
The young men tick like bombs in coffee bars,
Swallow the scalding music, pupils glow
Like fuses, dangerous. Yes, I suppose
They are quite capable of violent acts,
Translating into deed the feverish prose.
The odd thing is I've never seen them read,
Not wicked words nor any words at all,

As I've seen wrinkled gents and wispy dames
Munching up the print with serious greed,
The print recording deeds of lust and terror,
Incest, murder, rape and God knows what,
Intrepid readers who would squeak with horror
To see a mouse or dog or pussy bleed
And vomit at the sight of human snot.

VERNON SCANNELL

Brains for Hire

I went, expenses paid, to Stalin's Russia
and saw people's progress, which I recounted
in Oxford lectures and for the Left Book Club;
wrote socially conscious novels and burning
verse in Mayfair about Welsh mining valleys
from real conversations (my telephone bill
was prodigious) and recall good sales in Spain
and Sydney. That was my thirties period.

Brains for hire, brains for hire,
Hit the mood and find the buyer.

For a time I was undecided whether
to be a conchie in World War Two, but my
friends advised Intelligence, surmising – as
it turned out, rightly – this held material
for postwar thriller fiction. I was then switched
to Information and transformed the nation's
cuddly bears from Teddy to 'Uncle Joe', for
which I got the Royal Victorian (fourth class).

Brains for hire, brains for hire,
Hit the mood and find the buyer.

After the war I sang, converted, of the
Free World, and denounced the rank conformity
and cynicism of international
communism in literary journals,
flung across Europe, which I founded, managed
and edited myself with American
foundation money. Foes named the CIA,
Were sued, apologized, settled out of court.

Brains for hire, brains for hire,
Hit the mood and find the buyer.

My novels caught the tone of sex, antiques and
violence at its zenith; my concrete verse was
read with electronic music, massed banjos
and a pneumatic drill on the BBC;
I cut out sections of the walls of well-known
West End toilets and proclaimed them as a new
art form which no one dared to challenge and were
sold to the New York Museum of Modern Art.

Brains for hire, brains for hire,
Hit the mood and find the buyer.

I shone with Franco's sunny Spain in tourist
brochures, and unearthed Saudi Arabia
as the world's most democratic country for
a sponsored supplement, covered the Queen to
Canada and the Pope to Fatima and
found both events equally moving, and hailed
tax evasion millionaires as national
philanthropists deserving a life peerage.

Brains for hire, brains for hire,
Hit the mood and find the buyer.

I was converted from Against to For the
Common Market, and from Canterbury to Rome,
when I moved up Fleet Street. I was careful to
read back numbers of the paper to find out
my views on the United Nations and the
Commonwealth, Nasser, Aden, the balance of
payments and devaluation. I sold my
volumes of Russell and praised South Vietnam.

Brains for hire, brains for hire,
Hit the mood and find the buyer.

I rescued the fallen cigarette market
By linking smoke with God, devised a whiter
than white campaign for the Nigerian High
Commissioner, was photographed in fireproof
pyjamas on a slumberland mattress with
a blonde reading the latest Kingsley Amis
for next week's *Sunday Times* colour supplement,
and coined the phrase, 'Take a trip to inner space'.

Brains for hire, brains for hire,
Hit the mood and find the buyer.

DAVID TRIBE

The Soldier's Reply to the Poet

('*Will it be so again?*')

So the Soldier replied to the Poet,
Oh yes! it will all be the same,
But a bloody sight worse, and you know it
Since you have a hand in the game:
And you'll be the first in the racket

To sell us a similar dope,
Wrapped up in a rosier packet,
But noosed with as cunning a rope.
You coin us the catchwords and phrases
For which to be slaughtered; and then,
While thousands are blasted to blazes,
Sit picking your nose with your pen.
We know what you're bursting to tell us,
By heart. It is all very fine.
We must swallow the Bait that you sell us
And pay for your Hook and your Line.
But his pride for a soldier suffices
Since someone must carry the can;
In war, or depression, or crisis,
It's what you expect of a man.
But when we have come to the Isthmus
That bridges the Slump to the War,
We shall contact a new Father Christmas
Like the one we contacted before,
Deploring the one he replaces
Like you do (it's part of the show!)
But with those same mincing grimaces
And that mealy old kisser we know!
And he'll patent a cheap cornucopia
For all that our purse can afford,
And rent us a flat in Utopia
With dreams for our lodgings and board.
And we'll hand in our Ammo and Guns
As we handed them in once before,
And he'll lock them up safe; till our sons
Are conscripted for Freedom once more.
We can die for our faith by the million
And laugh at our bruises and scars,
But hush! for the Poet-Civilian
Is weeping, between the cigars.
Mellifluous, sweeter than Cadbury's,
The M.O.I. Nightingale (Hush!)

Is lining his pockets with Bradburies
So his feelings come out with a rush,
For our woes are the cash in his kitty
When his voice he so kindly devotes
In sentiment, pathos and pity,
To bringing huge lumps to the throats
Of our widows, and sweethearts, and trollops,
Since it sells like hot cakes to the town
As he doles out the Goitre in dollops
And the public is gulping it down.
Oh well may he weep for the soldier
Who weeps at a guinea a tear,
For although his invention gets mouldier,
It keeps him his job in the rear.
When my Mrs the organ is wheeling
And my adenoids wheeze to the sky,
He will publish the hunger I'm feeling
And rake in his cheque with a sigh:
And when with a trayful of matches
And laces, you hawk in the street,
O comrades in tatters and patches,
Rejoice! since we're in for a treat:
For when we have died in the gutter
To safeguard his income and state,
Be sure that the Poet will utter
Some beautiful thoughts on our Fate!
ROY CAMPBELL

Cecil B. de Mille

Cecil B. de Mille,
Rather against his will,
Was persuaded to leave Moses
Out of 'The Wars of the Roses'.
NICHOLAS BENTLEY

I hold your Hand in Mine

I hold your hand in mine, dear,
I press it to my lips.
I take a healthy bite from
Your dainty finger tips.

My joy would be complete, dear,
If you were only here,
But still I keep your hand as
A precious souvenir.

The night you died I cut it off,
I really don't know why.
For now each time I kiss it, I
Get bloodstains on my tie.

I'm sorry now I killed you, for
Our love was something fine,
And till they come to get me, I
Shall hold your hand in mine.

TOM LEHRER

Variations on an Air

AFTER WALT WHITMAN

Me clairvoyant,
Me conscious of you, old camarado,
Needing no telescope, lorgnette, field-glass, opera-glass, myopic
    pince-nez,
Me piercing two thousand years with eye naked and not ashamed;
The crown cannot hide you from me;
Musty old feudal-heraldic trappings cannot hide you from me,

I perceive that you drink.
(I am drinking with you. I am as drunk as you are.)
I see you are inhaling tobacco, puffing, smoking, spitting
(I do not object to your spitting),
You prophetic of American largeness,
You anticipating the broad masculine manners of these States;
I see in you also there are movements, tremors, tears, desire for
    the melodious,
I salute your three violinists, endlessly making vibrations,
Rigid, relentless, capable of going on for ever;
They play my accompaniment; but I shall take no notice of any
    accompaniment;
I myself am a complete orchestra.
So long.

G. K. CHESTERTON

How They Do It

NO. I. MR H. BELLOC

At Martinmas, when I was born,
   Hey diddle, Ho diddle, Do,
There came a cow with a crumpled horn,
   Hey diddle, Ho diddle, Do.
She stood agape and said, 'My dear,
You're a very fine child for this time of year,
And I think you'll have a taste in beer,'
   Hey diddle, Ho diddle, Ho, do, do, do,
   Hey diddle, Ho diddle, Do.

A taste in beer I've certainly got,
   Hey diddle, Ho diddle, Do,
A very fine taste that the Jews have not,
   Hey diddle, Ho diddle, Do.

93

And though I travel on the hills of Spain,
And Val-Pont-Côte and Belle Fontaine,
With lusty lungs I shall still maintain
Hey diddle, Ho diddle, Ho, do, do, do,
Hey diddle, Ho diddle, Do.

So Sussex men, wherever you be,
Hey diddle, Ho diddle, Do,
I pray you sing this song with me,
Hey diddle, Ho diddle, Do;
That of all the shires she is the queen,
And they sell at the 'Chequers' at Chanctonbury Green
The very best beer that ever was seen.
Hey Dominus, Domine, Dominum, Domini,
Domino, Domino.

J. C. SQUIRE

Chard Whitlow

(Mr Eliot's Sunday evening postscript)

As we get older we do not get any younger.
Seasons return, and today I am fifty-five,
And this time last year I was fifty-four,
And this time next year I shall be sixty-two.
And I cannot say I should like (to speak for myself)
To see my time over again – if you can call it time:
Fidgeting uneasily under a draughty stair,
Or counting sleepless nights in the crowded tube.

There are certain precautions – though none of them very reliable –
Against the blast from bombs and the flying splinter,

But not against the blast from heaven, *vento dei venti*,
The wind within a wind unable to speak for wind;
And the frigid burnings of purgatory will not be touched
By any emollient.
                    I think you will find this put,
Better than I could ever hope to express it,
In the words of Kharma: 'It is, we believe,
Idle to hope that the simple stirrup-pump
Will extinguish hell.'
                    Oh, listeners,
And you especially who have turned off the wireless,
And sit in Stoke or Basingstoke listening appreciatively to the
    silence,
(Which is also the silence of hell) pray, not for your skins, but
    your souls.

And pray for me also under the draughty stair.
As we get older we do not get any younger.

And pray for Kharma under the holy mountain.

HENRY REED

Just a Smack at Auden

Waiting for the end, boys, waiting for the end.
What is there to be or do?
What's become of me or you?
Are we kind or are we true?
Sitting two and two, boys, waiting for the end.

Shall I build a tower, boys, knowing it will rend
Crack upon the hour, boys, waiting for the end?
Shall I pluck a flower, boys, shall I save or spend?
All turns sour, boys, waiting for the end.

Shall I send a wire, boys? Where is there to send?
All are under fire, boys, waiting for the end.
Shall I turn a sire, boys? Shall I choose a friend?
The fat is in the pyre, boys, waiting for the end.

Shall I make it clear, boys, for all to apprehend,
Those that will not hear, boys, waiting for the end,
Knowing it is near, boys, trying to pretend,
Sitting in cold fear, boys, waiting for the end?

Shall we send a cable, boys, accurately penned,
Knowing we are able, boys, waiting for the end,
Via the Tower of Babel, boys? Christ will not ascend.
He's hiding in his stable, boys, waiting for the end.

Shall we blow a bubble, boys, glittering to distend,
Hiding from our trouble, boys, waiting for the end?
When you build on rubble, boys, Nature will append
Double and re-double, boys, waiting for the end.

Shall we make a tale, boys, that things are sure to mend,
Playing bluff and hale, boys, waiting for the end?
It will be born stale, boys, stinking to offend,
Dying ere it fails, boys, waiting for the end.

Shall we all go wild, boys, waste and make them lend,
Playing at the child, boys, waiting for the end?
It has all been filed, boys, history has a trend,
Each of us enisled, boys, waiting for the end.

What was said by Marx, boys, what did he perpend?
No good being sparks, boys, waiting for the end.
Treason of the clerks, boys, curtains that descend,
Lights becoming darks, boys, waiting for the end.

Waiting for the end, boys, waiting for the end.
Not a chance of blend, boys, things have got to tend.
Think of those who bend, boys, think of how we wend,
Waiting for the end, boys, waiting for the end.

WILLIAM EMPSON

Commentary

COMMENTARY

11. MARGINALIA (W. H. Auden)
Conrad Lorenz, Austrian naturalist, author of *King Solomon's Ring*
and other books about animals, invites his readers to believe that much
in human society is to be interpreted in terms of animal behaviour. The
reference to 'pecking' is also an extrapolation from the behaviour of
hens.

13. A POLITICIAN (e. e. cummings)
In America the term 'politician' has a somewhat wider significance
than in Britain, where '*party* politician' is implied. The American sense
is almost that of a 'manipulator'.

**13. ON READING THE WAR DIARY OF A DEFUNCT
AMBASSADOR (Siegfried Sassoon)**
Beneath the urbane and controlled surface of Sassoon's satire there
is always a basis of genuine anger and indignation.

14. 'NEXT TO OF COURSE GOD' (e. e. cummings)
Cummings (who, like Sassoon, was a combatant in World War I)
makes excellent use here of the apparently incoherent poetic style he
invented: this poem directly reflects the real meaninglessness of war-
mongering rhetoric and incorporates snatches of American patriotic
songs.

15. AT THE BANK IN SPAIN (D. H. Lawrence)
Even in Catholic countries, Lawrence is saying, the priests themselves
join in the universal homage to money.

16. A CIVIL SERVANT (Robert Graves)
A fanciful portrait satirizing the alleged rocklike passivity of the
average civil servant.

17. A TRIBUTE TO THE FOUNDER (Kingsley Amis)

The implication is that corruption is ineradicable, manifesting itself even in a new university. Is this fair?

17. PLANNING PERMISSION (James Reeves)

The lines 'with relief I saw that he at least had had his due reward' (i.e. promotion) underline the implication that it is the same person who interviews the applicant on each successive occasion. It is to the credit of one local government department that, when this piece appeared in *The Listener*, it was pinned up on the notice-board of the Leicester City planning department.

19. WAS IT NOT CURIOUS? (Stevie Smith)

One version of the legend here referred to is that, before he became Pope, Gregory I, seeing some fair-haired youths in the slave-market in Rome, enquired of what nation they were. On being told that they were English (Angli), he punningly replied, 'Not Angli but Angeli if they become Christians.' Soon after he became Pope, he sent Augustine on a missionary journey to convert the English. St Augustine (A.D. 604) became the first Archbishop of Canterbury.

19. THE HIPPOPOTAMUS (T. S. Eliot)

Eliot here contrasts the True Church (i.e. the official Christian establishment), which is theoretically strong and infallible, with the hippopotamus, which is frail and helpless. By an ironic reversal of rôles the hippo is in the end given Christ's blessing and receives salvation. The suggestion of worldliness and laxity in the modern Church is reinforced by the epigraph from St Paul's Epistle to the Colossians, IV. The Laodiceans were an early Christian sect who, as can be seen from Revelations III, were 'lukewarm', worldly and prosperous. The Latin quotation from St Ignatius concerns the organization of the Church and means: 'In like manner, let all reverence the Deacons as Jesus Christ and the Bishop as the Father, and the Presbyters as the council of God, and the assembly of the Apostles. Without these there is no Church. Concerning all which I am persuaded that ye think after the same manner.'

21. IN THE CEMETERY (Thomas Hardy)

This, together with *In Church* (p. 21), comes from a group of poems which Hardy called *Satires of Circumstance*.

23. FOUNDER'S FEAST (Siegfried Sassoon)
A Regius Professor is usually venerable and appointed by royal mandate. *Provost:* principal or other important functionary at an institution of learning. The college here referred to is evidently King's, Cambridge.

25. SONGS OF EDUCATION: THE CRECHE (G. K. Chesterton)
A satire against what would now be called Day Nurseries.

26. APOLLO OF THE PHYSIOLOGISTS (Robert Graves)
As in *The Eugenist* (p. 24), Graves makes fun of science, here exemplified by the typical medical textbook. Physiologists, he says, deny that they either accept or reject the notion of God, or of some scientific substitute for God; but a male being in the likeness of the Greek god Apollo is depicted everywhere (*passim*) in their textbooks.

27. BASE DETAILS (Siegfried Sassoon)
The anger and scorn here expressed were more appropriate at the time of World War I, when Sassoon wrote, than at that of the 1939 war.

28. THE PERSIAN VERSION (Robert Graves)
The defeat of the Persians at the Battle of Marathon (490 B.C.) by the Greeks under Miltiades was one of the most decisive and important events in ancient history. Graves's ironic version of the facts, by which an imaginary Persian commentator seeks to minimize their defeat, satirizes notorious and laughable attempts by British military spokesmen during the early part of World War II to write off resounding British failures against the Germans in order to maintain morale.

29. LESSONS OF THE WAR (Henry Reed)
The epigraph from one of the *Odes* of Horace occurs in the following context: 'Though that life is past, I *was lately still fit for war and fought my battles not without glory.* Now my armour and my lute, whose campaigns are over, will hang on yonder wall.' (Some scholars read 'puellis' instead of 'duellis'.)
Henry Reed's justly celebrated *Lessons of the War* are the best English satires to have come out of the 1939 war. They are more than

satire; they are true satirical poetry, a rare form. As satire they are amusing pastiches of the typical army instructor – technically equipped, conscientious, humane, his knowledge of army jargon considerably outrunning his handling of English syntax. On this level Reed does not sneer at the instructor; he scarcely deviates into parody. 'On se moque toujours de ce qu'on aime', and Reed has too much sympathy with the instructor in his situation as one training conscripted recruits for battle, to display his own superiority. He merely selects from the instructor's discourses, underlines here and there by repetition, and lets the words speak for themselves.

But as poems the *Lessons* rise above the purely satirical. The lyrical passages in *Naming of Parts*, for instance, counterpoint the instructor's discourse and insist on the esoteric sexual symbolism in the discourse – a symbolism of which, ironically, the instructor is quite unaware, but which is part of the common – indeed, the folk – experience of all young men. ('The early bees are assaulting and fumbling the flowers.') *Judging Distances* and *Movement of Bodies* are more purely comic, and pursue the same theme: the personal frustrations of the sex-starved recruit having to endure the painfully subliterate speech of the instructor.

34. THE FLYING BUM: 1944 (William Plomer)
Plomer's small book of satirical poems, *The Dorking Thigh*, is among the very best satire of this century. He is at his wittiest and most pointed when making fun of cranks. In 1944 the Germans attacked southern England with a new terror weapon, the unmanned flying bomb, launched from the coast of occupied France. Its military effect was small, but its damage to British morale was considerable. The vegetarians, like others, were under the necessity of using many substitutes for their normal healthy diet.

36. DRY AUGUST BURNED (Walter de la Mare)
This is satire in its most serious sense: the effect of war on the innocent arouses de la Mare's bitterest anger. (See introduction, where it is pointed out that satire does not necessarily involve an element of ridicule.)

41. HOW BEASTLY THE BOURGEOIS IS (D. H. Lawrence)
Since Lawrence wrote this over forty years ago, the word 'bourgeois' has acquired wide meanings as a term of abuse for almost any way of

life the user objects to, does not share, or perhaps only aspires to. Lawrence evidently defines it as the way of life of a social class, the class which goes shooting and golfing. It is worth considering whether the word has any real meaning three centuries after it was first used by the French to distinguish the mercantile and shopkeeping town-dweller from the peasant or landed gentleman. A later definition is 'addicted to comfort and respectability, humdrum'.

42. HUMANITY I LOVE YOU (e. e. cummings)

This perhaps offers a different view of the bourgeois mentality. *The old howard:* a music hall in Boston.

43. THE WORLD STATE (G. K. Chesterton)

A typical Chestertonian attack on minority groups who do not practise what they preach.

44 THE FIRM OF HAPPINESS LIMITED (Norman Cameron)

The false optimism of the between-wars period ending in 1939 is here satirized, universal 'Happiness' being objectified as a vast department store gone bankrupt. *Bourse:* Paris Stock Exchange.

45. THE DORKING THIGH (William Plomer)

See note above (p. 104) on *The Flying Bum.* This re-enactment of a typical newspaper sensation suggests the unexplained horror that may lurk behind the façade of bourgeois respectability. Dorking in Surrey is taken as the type of gin-belt commuter land.

47. THE OXFORD VOICE (D. H. Lawrence)

This voice is perhaps less prominent, at any rate in Oxford, than in D. H. Lawrence's time, but it can still be heard in the right places.

47. HOW TO GET ON IN SOCIETY (John Betjeman)

Nancy Mitford wrote an amusing and deliberately snobbish account of what she and her upper-class friends called 'U and non-U'. The 'non-U' (i.e. 'non-upper') things in ordinary life were those not used or not referred to by the 'best' people, among whom it was simply not done to talk about 'fish-knives', 'doileys', etc. Betjeman won a weekend magazine competition for the best piece of verse containing as many non-U expressions as possible.

48. THE FECKLESS DINNER PARTY (Walter de la Mare)
De la Mare expresses his contempt and hatred for people of this kind – mean, spiteful and tattling – by imagining them guided down to hell instead of to dinner by the new butler Toomes.

50. THE BRITISH WORKMAN AND THE GOVERNMENT (D. H. Lawrence)
Lawrence, always proud of his working-class origin, was exasperated in the 1920s by what he thought of as the passivity of his class in accepting unemployment and bad working conditions. The workers are now considerably more militant, and the change in the general social climate is due, at least in part, to such writers as Lawrence.

51. CHICO AND THE PRISON DOCTORS (Tim Daly)
Daly wrote his poems in prison.

52. A BALLAD OF THE GOOD LORD NELSON (Lawrence Durrell)
Durrell is preaching that Nelson should be regarded more as a sex hero than a naval one. *Stylites:* St Simeon Stylites was a fifth-century saint who spent the last thirty-six years of his life on the top of a column in an unsuccessful attempt to get away from the crowds of those who came to seek him for his sanctity.

53. THE RUINED MAID (Thomas Hardy)
Two country girls meet and discuss the change in appearance and manners of one of them, Amelia, who, tired of the boredom and hard work associated with farm life, has gone to town as the mistress of a man of means. In the eyes of the respectable she is 'ruined'.

54. THE CONFORMERS (Thomas Hardy)
An ironical comment on conventional marriage with obvious autobiographical implications: Hardy's own first marriage was not a success.

57. THE HABITS (Louis MacNeice)
In this effectively light-handed satire on the five ages of conventional man it is only stanza 3 that is not quite clear. As the habits take temporary leave of the man, they launch a Parthian (i.e. backwards over the shoulder) arrow and deliver a signed statement. It is not clear what the statement is – possibly of an intention to return. Or could it be

connected with an impending divorce? The adgirl is presumably the bride – a conventional girl like those in advertisements. Or possibly the co-respondent?

58. REQUEST ON THE FIELD (Martin Seymour-Smith)
In this light-heartedly rueful poem the author is replying to a friend or mentor who has urged him to conform to the rules of the game, which of course is life rather than football. In the final line he says 'What is the point of it all With what does one score the goals of success?'

61. DEATH OF AN ACTRESS (Louis MacNeice)
A sympathetic portrait of an actual vaudeville singer whose popularity was due largely to her ability to fulfil the nostalgic public demand for sentimental escape from routine and boredom. According to the folk ballad on which the pantomime *The Babes in the Wood* was based, the lost babes were protected from the cold because the birds covered them with fallen leaves.

62. THE PLAYBOY OF THE DEMI-WORLD: 1938
(William Plomer)
A ruthless but not unsympathetic picture of an ageing homosexual entertaining others like himself. He is rich (his flat is in Mayfair, London's most expensive residential area) and he lives entirely for frivolous amusement and to fight off loneliness – fiddling while Rome burns (1938 was the year of the Munich settlement that made the 1939 war inevitable). The portrait, though over thirty years old, is in no way dated. Line 4 is an inspired parody of the famous 'A rose-red city half as old as time' in the Victorian poem *Petra* by the Rev. John William Burgon. *Saurian:* of the zoological order of lizards, including crocodiles, alligators, etc., many of them noted for longevity. *Aunts:* one of the many cant terms for homosexuals. *Ganymede:* a beautiful youth, cup-bearer to Jupiter.

63. SLOUGH (John Betjeman)
Slough, in South Buckinghamshire, grew up without beauty of design after World War I round a trading estate for light industry formed from an ex-War Office arms dump. The trading estate has always been known locally as 'the Dump'. Not only is this deplorable town in the midst of the beautiful country between Burnham Beeches

and the Thames at Eton, but it has swallowed up some charming houses and villages. Betjeman has done much for the cause of conservation, and the effectiveness of his satire is due largely to the anger which comes through it. His exaggerations are forgivable, because the spoliation of natural and architectural beauty has always moved him to passionate indignation. This is the kind of satire we still need.

65. '¡WELLCOME, TO THE CAVES OF ARTÁ!' (Robert Graves)
Graves has lived in Majorca for most of the second half of his life. He has always resented the increasing exploitation of the island by the tourist industry. Under an appearance of good-humoured parody, this poem is an angry one. It is headed by an actual quotation from a Spanish tourist brochure in execrable English, and Graves continues in the same style.

66. WELCOME TO WALES (R. S. Thomas)
The rigours of the pound's climate: England, where money is made.

68. RESORT (R. S. Thomas)
A once popular sentimental song is entitled 'What are the wild waves saying?'. English factory workers come to a Welsh seaside resort, possibly Llandudno. The final question implies that English visitors expect the sea on the Welsh coast to speak English as well as Welsh.

68. NO OFFENCE (D. J. Enright)
A somewhat sick account of Germany's noted efficiency. *Lufthansa:* the German state airline.

70. THE NORTH (Brian Higgins)
This very promising poet, who died prematurely, was himself from the working class.

71. ROMANCE OF A YOUNGEST DAUGHTER
(John Crowe Ransom)
A shrewdly humorous comment on the kind of society, evidently of some period in the past, in which daughters were 'married off' to eligible suitors.

72. AN IMPORTER (Robert Frost)
A satire against the American tourist who returns home laden with oriental nicknacks and repeating oriental strictures on the American way of life, especially the destructive tendencies of mass-production. The final line refers to the colloquial expression 'Go and teach your grandmother to suck eggs' addressed to anyone telling the speaker how to do something he has long known how to do.

73. COME, GAZE WITH ME (e. e. cummings)
A bitterly ironical contrasting of the reality and the ideals of upper-class American patriotism in time of war.

74. AMERICANIZATION (G. K. Chesterton)
Chesterton's patriotism now strikes us as a little dated, but he was a staunch fighter for lost or unpopular causes.

79. THE LAUREATE (Robert Graves)
A hate poem against Robert Bridges (note pun in line 2), who was Poet Laureate from 1913 till his death in 1930. *Heliotropic:* light-seeking.

79. MR NIXON (Ezra Pound)
Pound composed this presentation of a thoroughly worldly and successful author giving advice to an idealistic beginner in the person of his self-presentation as Hugh Selwyn Mauberley. The original of Mr Nixon is supposed to have been the novelist Arnold Bennett, well known for his avarice and his love of material pleasures. He owned a steam yacht, of which he was very proud. Pound's contempt for him was complete; however, Bennett wrote some very good novels. It should be added that Pound was generous with good advice to young writers. *Dr Dundas:* presumably either a publisher or a hostile critic. *Bloughram:* the worldly, time-serving priest of Browning's *Bishop Bloughram's Apology. The Nineties:* some poets of the 1890s believed idealistically in poverty and 'art for art's sake'.

80. MUSEUMS (Louis MacNeice)
MacNeice sees museums as places where we hide from reality by living vicariously the lives of the dead.

81. THE APOLOGY OF BOTTOM THE WEAVER
(G. K. Chesterton)

A typical piece of mockery against 'modern' fashions in the form of a commentary on the dream of Bottom the weaver. (For the references to the four fairies see *A Midsummer Night's Dream* III.i.) Chesterton neatly introduces into his nine stanzas several of his favourite prejudices – against excessive surgery (commonly practised in his time), vegetarianism, psychoanalysis and motor transport which destroys rural life, as well as his prejudice in favour of craft skills. On a more serious controversial level the poem is a plea for a magical, as distinct from a rationalistic, view of life. *Fair science frowned not on his birth:* quoted, ironically, from the Epitaph at the end of Gray's Elegy.

82. PERSONALITY CULT (James Reeves)

This satire was caused by irritation at the gossipy type of radio 'portrait' too often put out by the BBC, such as the one on Henry James. *Gath and Askelon:* cities of the Philistines, regarded as types of anti-culture.

83. SPICER'S INSTANT POETRY (James Reeves)

This attack on bad contemporary poetry was turned down regretfully by the editor of a leading literary magazine on the ground that it sounded as if it was getting at much of the poetry published in his magazine.

84. BERNARD SHAW (E. C. Bentley)

Shaw has seldom been accused of physical or moral cowardice, but his eagerness to make money was notorious.

84. SURVEY OF LITERATURE (John Crowe Ransom)

This *tour de force* of gastronomic characterization is aimed at the type of literary criticism which maintains that poets are concerned solely with language rather than the stuff of physical life and the means of getting it. The title of the poem suggests the kind of academic critical writing that Ransom is satirizing.

85. GENERATION OF A CRITIC (James Reeves)

The title contains a reference to Dryden's remark. 'The corruption of a poet is the generation of a critic' (Dedication to the *Examen Poeticum*).

87. BRAINS FOR HIRE (David Tribe)

A cuttingly ironical account of the career of a 'progressive' intellectual from the thirties to the present day. The Left Book Club, run by the astute publisher Victor Gollancz in the 1930s, exploited fashionably leftish interests and movements. This was the period of parlour Communism. In World War II the composite hero of the poem, overcoming his doctrinal objections to a 'capitalistic' war, serves first in the Intelligence Service, and then in the Ministry of Information, receiving a decoration for composing propaganda for the Russia of Joseph Stalin, Britain's ally against Germany. He next finds it profitable to join the crusade against international Communism. (The progressive magazine *Encounter* is said to have been subsidized by dollars from the anti-Communist Central Intelligence Agency of America.) More recently he is found cashing in on the demand for sex and avant-garde music, poetry and art. He is then paid by reactionary foreign régimes to create public interest in tourism. A further series of unsavoury assignments enriches him, and he ends by doing anything and everything for money and publicity.

89. THE SOLDIER'S REPLY TO THE POET (Roy Campbell)

Campbell, a combatant in both world wars, bitterly attacks the poets employed as propagandists for war. (See previous poem, stanza 2.)

91. CECIL B. DE MILLE (Nicholas Bentley)

Nicholas Bentley is the son of Edmund Clerihew Bentley, who invented the 'clerihew', which is the form of the present lampoon on the very dubious historical accuracy of the late de Mille's mammoth film epics of life in ancient times. The lampoon on Bernard Shaw (p. 83) by the elder Bentley is also a 'clerihew'.

92. I HOLD YOUR HAND IN MINE (Tom Lehrer)

Much of Tom Lehrer's verse is not, essentially, sick or cynical but is a healthy comment on certain types of popular song, of which he is an acute and effective critic. The present example is a send-up of the sugary love lyric of the popular crooner. Unfortunately for the purpose of this anthology, and fortunately for those who enjoy Lehrer's records, the piano settings, brilliantly composed and executed by the singer himself, are an integral part of his songs.

92. VARIATIONS ON AN AIR: AFTER WALT WHITMAN
(G. K. Chesterton)

A parody of the style of Walt Whitman, who is here represented retrospectively as addressing Old King Cole.

93. HOW THEY DO IT: HILAIRE BELLOC (J. C. Squire)

Squire, the once well-known literary editor, was not much of a poet himself, but had a good knowledge of the poetry of some of his contemporaries. The best fruit of this, and the best of his verse, is *Tricks of the Trade*, examples of what he calls 'the not wholly admirable art' of parody. Here he hits off, with almost cruel perceptiveness, Belloc's hearty ballad style with its crude, insistent metrical beat. The neat transformation of the nonsensical refrain in the final stanza reminds us of Belloc's fanatical devotion to the Roman Catholic Church – a devotion which also made him anti-semitic. (See stanza 2 line 3.) He was of French descent and upbringing. Another feature of Belloc's writing noticed by Squire is his love of the 'ye olde', beer in quantity, Sussex, and walking tours through Catholic Europe.

94. CHARD WHITLOW (Henry Reed)

This brilliant parody of T. S. Eliot's manner at the time of World War II won a *New Statesman* competition and the admiration of Eliot himself. Admittedly, the very mannered style of the *Four Quartets* is not difficult to take off, but that only makes it easier for the second-rate parodist. What is especially to Reed's credit is that he makes something really funny out of an imitation of something very serious indeed. Reed greatly admires Eliot, but he is sufficiently detached to be well aware of Eliot's tendency to utter platitudinous truisms, to adopt a pedantic diction, to quote Italian, to harp on the theme of time, and to air his High Anglicanism and his interest in oriental philosophy. Eliot was a tall and very dignified person, and the idea of his crouching under a draughty stair during London air-raids is a happy one. At this time the BBC used to put out radio 'postscripts' by well-known people after the Sunday evening news bulletins, with the general idea of boosting civilian morale. The title of this parody refers to an imaginary village near Chard in Somerset and echoes such titles in the *Four Quartets* as *Little Gidding* and *East Coker*, and the subtitle reminds us of Eliot's early poem *Mr Eliot's Sunday Morning Service*.

95. JUST A SMACK AT AUDEN (William Empson)

Empson is one of Auden's most gifted contemporaries, a subtle poet as well as an acute critic of literature. This is not a verbal parody of Auden's style; it is a satirical re-working of some of the ideas current among the fashionable poets of the 1930s, whose theoretical Marxism and parlour revolutionary talk had a wide appeal among the younger of the intelligentsia. The reference in stanza 9 to 'treason of the clerks' recalls the influential French book by Julien Benda *La Tragison des Clercs* (1927), attacking the reactionary tendencies of certain intellectuals.

ACKNOWLEDGEMENTS

The editor and publishers wish to thank the following for permission to reprint copyright material: Mr M. B. Yeats and Macmillan & Co. Ltd for 'The Scholars' by W. B. Yeats from *The Collected Poems*; Faber and Faber Ltd for 'When statesmen gravely say' from *Collected Shorter Poems 1927-57* and six verses from 'Marginalia' from *City without Walls* by W. H. Auden; Constable & Co. Ltd for 'On the Birth of his Son' from *170 Chinese Poems* translated by Arthur Waley; MacGibbon & Kee for 'a politician is an arse upon', 'next to of course god america i', 'humanity i love you' and 'come gaze with me upon this dome' by e. e. cummings from the *Collected Poems*; Mr G. T. Sassoon for 'They', 'Founders Feast', 'On Reading the War Diary of a Defunct Ambassador', 'Does it Matter?' and 'Base Details' by Siegfried Sassoon; Laurence Pollinger Ltd and the Estate of the Late Mrs Frieda Lawrence for 'At the Bank in Spain', 'The British Workman and the Government', 'Wales', 'The Mosquito knows', 'The Oxford Voice' and 'How Beastly the Bourgeois is' by D. H. Lawrence from *The Complete Poems*; Alfred Knopf/Random House Inc. and Eyre and Spottiswoode for 'Romance of a Youngest Daughter' and 'Survey of Literature' by John Crowe Ransom from *Selected Poems*; Robert Graves for '¡Wellcome, to the Caves of Artá!', 'A Civil Servant', 'Apollo of the Physiologists' and 'The Eugenist' from *Collected Poems 1955* and for 'The Persian Version' and 'The Laureate' from *Collected Poems 1965*; Jonathan Cape Ltd and Henry Reed for 'Naming of Parts' and 'Judging Distances' from 'Lessons of War', and 'Chad Whitlow' from *A Map of Verona*; Henry Reed for 'Movement of Bodies' from 'Lessons of War'; Jonathan Cape Ltd and William Plomer for 'The Flying Bum: 1944', 'The Playboy of the Demi-World: 1938' and 'The Dorking Thigh' from *Collected Poems*; Jonathan Cape Ltd and the Estate of Robert Frost for 'An Importer' from *The Poetry of Robert Frost* edited by Edward Connery Lathem; Jonathan Cape Ltd and Kingsley Amis for 'A Tribute to the Founder' and 'Aberdarcy: the Main Square' from *A Look Round the Estate*; James Reeves and William Heinemann Ltd for 'Planning Permission', 'Spicer's Instant Poetry' and 'Generation of a Critic' from *The Questioning Tiger* and for 'Personality Cult'; Longman Group Ltd for 'Was it not Curious' by Stevie Smith from *Selected Poems*; Faber & Faber Ltd for 'The Hippopotamus' by T. S. Eliot from *Collected Poems 1909-1962*; Macmillan & Co. Ltd and the Trustees of the Hardy Estate for 'The Ruined Maid', 'In Church', 'In the Cemetery', 'The Conformers' and 'The Lady in the

Furs' by Thomas Hardy from *Collected Poems*; Mr Raglan Squire for 'How They do It: Mr H. Belloc' by J. C. Squire; The Fortune Press for 'Cambridge' by Gavin Ewart from *Poems and Songs*; Abelard-Schuman and Martin Seymour-Smith for 'What Schoolmasters Say' and 'Request on the Field' from *Tea with Miss Stockport*; Miss D. F. Collins and Methuen & Co. Ltd for 'Songs of Education: for the Creche', 'The World State', 'Americanization', 'The Apology of Bottom the Weaver' and 'Variations on an Air: after Walt Whitman' by G. K. Chesterton from *Collected Poems*; The Literary Trustees of Walter de la Mare and the Society of Authors as their representative for 'Dry August Burned', 'The Feckless Dinner Party' and 'Hi' from *Complete Poems*; The Hogarth Press and the Literary Estate of Norman Cameron for 'The Firm of Happiness Limited' from *Collected Poems*; John Betjeman and John Murray Ltd for 'How to get on in Society' and 'Slough' from *Collected Poems*; Tim Daly for 'Chico and the Prison Doctors'; Faber and Faber Ltd for 'A Ballad of the Good Lord Nelson' by Lawrence Durrell from *Collected Poems*, for 'The Habits', 'Death of an Actress' and 'Museums' by Louis Mac-Neice from *The Collected Poems*, for 'Mr Nixon' by Ezra Pound from *Collected Shorter Poems*, and for 'Just a Smack at Auden' by William Empson from *The Gathering Storm*; R. S. Thompson and Rupert Hart-Davis for 'Welcome to Wales' and 'Resort' by R. S. Thomas from *Not That He Brought Flowers*; D. J. Enright and Chatto & Windus Ltd for 'No Offence' from *Selected Poems*; Abelard-Schuman and Brian Higgins for extract from 'The North' from *The Only Need*; Oxford University Press for 'A Word in Edgeways' from *The Way of a World* by Charles Tomlinson © Oxford University Press 1969; The Estate of E. C. Bentley for 'Bernard Shaw' from *Clerihews Complete*; Vernon Scannell for 'The Wicked Words'; David Tribe for 'Brains for Hire'; The Estate of Roy Campbell for 'The Soldier's Reply to the Poet' from *Adamastor*; Nicolas Bentley for 'Cecil B. de Mille'; Paul Elek Ltd for 'I hold your hand in mine' by Tom Lehrer from *The Tom Lehrer Song Book*.

INDEX OF TITLES AND FIRST LINES

INDEX OF AUTHORS